CORPORATE TAX REFORM

TAXING PROFITS IN THE 21ST CENTURY

Martin A. Sullivan

Apress®

Corporate Tax Reform: Taxing Profits in the 21st Century

Copyright © 2011 by Martin A. Sullivan

ISBN-13 (pbk): 978-1-4302-3927-7

ISBN-13 (electronic): 978-1-4302-3928-4

Trademarked names may appear in this book. Rather than use a trademark symbol with every occurrence of a trademarked name, we use the names only in an editorial fashion and to the benefit of the trademark owner, with no intention of infringement of the trademark.

Lead Editor: Jeff Olson
Technical Reviewer: George White
Editorial Board: Steve Anglin, Mark Beckner, Ewan Buckingham, Gary Cornell, Morgan Engel, Jonathan Gennick, Jonathan Hassell, Robert Hutchinson, Michelle Lowman, James Markham, Matthew Moodie, Jeff Olson, Jeffrey Pepper, Douglas Pundick, Ben Renow-Clarke, Dominic Shakeshaft, Gwenan Spearing, Matt Wade, Tom Welsh
Coordinating Editor: Adam Heath
Copy Editor: Damon Larson
Compositor: Mary Sudul
Indexer: SPi Global
Cover Designer: Anna Ishschenko

Distributed to the book trade worldwide by Springer-Verlag New York, Inc., 233 Spring Street, 6th Floor, New York, NY 10013. Phone 1-800-SPRINGER, fax 201-348-4505, e-mail orders-ny@springer-sbm.com, or visit www.springeronline.com.

For information on translations, please contact us by e-mail at info@apress.com, or visit www.apress.com.

Apress and friends of ED books may be purchased in bulk for academic, corporate, or promotional use. eBook versions and licenses are also available for most titles. For more information, reference our Special Bulk Sales–eBook Licensing web page at www.apress.com/bulk-sales. To place an order, email your request to support@apress.com

For Mary

Contents

About the Author

Martin A. Sullivan is an economist and contributing editor for Tax Analysts, a nonprofit publisher of *Tax Notes*, *Tax Notes International*, and *State Tax Notes* in Falls Church, Virginia. His passion for economics began when he had trouble finding a job during the great recession of 1973-74. He graduated magna cum laude from Harvard College and received a Ph.D. in economics from Northwestern University. He taught economics at Rutgers University and then served as a staff economist, first at the Office of Tax Analysis at the U.S. Department of Treasury and then at the congressional Joint Committee on Taxation. He has also worked as a self-employed economic consultant and an economist at a major accounting firm. For the last 15 years, he has written over 500 economic analyses for Tax Analysts publications and is a regular contributor to the www.tax.com blog. He has testified before Congress on numerous occasions and is frequently quoted in major print publications and often appears on television. Recently, he was interviewed by Leslie Stahl on CBS's *60 Minutes*. He lives in Alexandria, Virginia with his wife, Mary, and two children, Laura and Joseph.

About the
Technical Reviewer

George White is a *Tax Notes* contributing editor and retired national tax partner at Ernst & Young LLP. Recently he was with the American Institute of Certified Public Accountants. He is the author of several publications on consolidated returns and tax accounting and is an adjunct professor at the George Washington University School of Business, where he teaches graduate courses in tax accounting and corporate tax. White is an attorney and CPA.

Introduction:
Before We Begin

A Little Bit of History

January 1983 was a gloomy time at the Reagan White House. The president had promised his 1981 tax cuts would deliver prosperity. But instead the nation was suffering from the worst recession since the days of Herbert Hoover. The unemployment rate was over 10 percent. The Republican gains won in the House of Representatives in 1980 were wiped out in the midterm elections. The president's approval rating had dropped to 35 percent. The Reagan Revolution was in deep trouble.

It was not just the sagging economy that was pummeling the Reagan presidency. It was the perception that his policies favored the privileged classes. He was being branded as a champion of the rich. The tax cuts were sold to the public as benefiting everybody because the wealthy and the large corporations who got most of the direct benefit would create jobs. Now where were the jobs? Even his own budget director called the tax cuts "a Trojan horse" designed to convince the American public that they were getting a gift when "in reality the plan was designed to reduce the taxes of the rich and super rich."[1] On top of all that, the massive tax cuts that were supposed to be self-financing were producing the largest deficits since World War II.

Above all else, politicians need to empathize with the voters. Bill Clinton's "I feel your pain" response to unemployed workers during the 1992 campaign is a textbook example. In the dark days of early 1983, Reagan needed to demonstrate his concern for the poor and for middle-class workers who were bearing the brunt of the recession. Traditionally

---

[1] William Greider, "The Education of David Stockman," *Atlantic Monthly*, www.theatlantic.com/magazine/archive/1981/12/the-education-of-david-stockman/5760/, December 1981.

Democratic working-class northerners had been the pivotal swing voters in his stunning 1980 victory.

So the White House staff dispatched the president to Massachusetts to do what he did best. The television image the White House wanted on the evening news was of Ronnie hoisting a cold one with his fellow Irish Americans at the working-class Eire Pub in Dorchester. The pub visit was a resounding success. The lunchtime crowd, mostly Democratic, was charmed. Around the horseshoe bar they were photographed with the president cheerily raising a mug of Ballantine ale.

But those pictures of political perfection never made it to prime time. That evening, all three major networks reported Reagan's remarks made after his pub visit to business executives in suburban Boston's high-tech corridor. And they made the exact opposite impression his White House handlers were hoping to project. Despite the advance scripting of both the speaker and his audience, the president surprised everybody when he ventured from his prepared text. "When are we all going to have the courage to point out that, in our tax structure, the corporate tax is very hard to justify?" he asked the executives assembled in a company cafeteria. The president knew he was playing with fire—"I'll probably kick myself for having said this"—and he tried to explain that he believed his idea would help workers' pension funds heavily invested in stock—but it was no use.[2] The cat was out of the bag. At a time when nearly 12 million Americans were enduring the pain of unemployment, the president was proposing to relieve large U.S. corporations of their entire tax burden.

The Democrats and the press had a field day. "On the same day the president sat down with the working men of Boston—and I have no complaint about that whatsoever—he showed that his heart was still in the corporate board room," said House Speaker Tip O'Neill, Democrat from Massachusetts.[3] White House press secretary Larry Speakes complained the press was going "berserk" and "doing back flips." Privately, the White House staff was alarmed by the president's off-the-cuff comments. Publicly they did all they could to squelch the story. Speakes paraphrased the president as saying

[2] Ronald Reagan, "Remarks and a Question-and-Answer Session with Members of the Massachusetts High Technology Council in Bedford," www.reagan.utexas.edu/archives/speeches/1983/12683e.htm, January 26, 1983.

[3] Benjamin Taylor, "Kill Corporate Income Tax? No Way, Say Reagan Aides," *Boston Globe*, January 28, 1983.

on the flight back from Boston, "I do not want anyone to look into it."[4] The official message: No, it was not a real proposal. End of story.

Deft damage control by the president's staff played a large part in getting the story off the front pages. But there was another contributing factor. Follow-up press coverage revealed that for all the political controversy, there was nothing startling in the president's remarks to policy experts and economists. Unlike so many other proposals from Reagan that ignited heated debate in the economics profession, the abolition of the corporation tax was not one of them.

In the *National Journal*, commentator Robert Samuelson called the corporate tax a "self-inflicted wound" that is "popular because corporations are un-popular."[5] *Business Week* columnist Norman Jonas wrote that "fundamental reform of the corporate income tax is neither a liberal nor a conservative idea. It is a matter of economic efficiency and social equity, with proponents on both sides of the political divide."[6] Economists of all stripes agreed with the president: the corporate tax imposed a second layer of tax on corporate profits and had no economic justification. Liberals did not like hearing econo-mists agree with Reagan. And with an election approaching, conservatives did not want to remind the public of Reagan's natural inclination to cut corporate taxes. The story faded from view.

In the following months, the economy and Reagan's approval would steadily rise. The upswing culminated in a sweeping victory over former Vice Presi-dent Mondale, whose own frankness about taxes—in particular, about raising taxes—contributed to his electoral defeat.

In the relative political security of his second term, Reagan achieved what many thought was impossible: a top-to-bottom overhaul of the Internal Revenue Code. The original plan from his Treasury Department seemed to reflect the sentiments the president expressed in Massachusetts on that Janu-ary afternoon of 1983. It included a provision to partially eliminate the double tax on corporate profits. But that item was dropped in the early stages of the legislative process as Reagan and Congress pursued other priorities.

The president and congressional leaders agreed that tax reform would be revenue-neutral—overall, the legislation would neither raise nor cut taxes.

---

[4] Francis X. Clines, "Corporate Tax Upsets Reagan," *New York Times*, January 26, 1983.

[5] Robert J. Samuelson, "Self-Inflicted Wound," *National Journal*, February 5, 1983.

[6] *Norman Jonas*, "That Wasn't Really a Gaffe on *Corporate Taxes*," *Business Week*, February 14, *1983*.

As the bill wound its way through Congress, it became necessary to cut taxes on individuals. This shortfall had to be made up with tax increases on business. The final plan adopted by Congress in the Tax Reform Act of 1986 included a corporate rate reduction from 46 to 34 percent. But extensive cutbacks to corporate tax credits and deductions more than offset the benefit of the rate cuts. The act raised the tax burden on corporations. In less than four years, Reagan had gone from advocate of abolishing the corporate tax to signing into law a major increase in corporate taxes.

Reagan's dramatic reversal on corporate taxes is a perfect illustration of the fundamental paradox of the corporate tax in American politics. There are many liberal economists who argue that the corporate tax should be abolished. But even the most conservative politicians are reluctant to back up their anti-corporate tax rhetoric with decisive action. The corporation tax is a political minefield even for the most agile politicians. Experts can profess the need to eliminate double taxation of corporate profits until they are blue in the face. But popular sentiment against corporate tax cuts is a far more potent political force.

More than a quarter-century after Reagan's signing the Tax Reform Act of 1986, the basic political forces that have shaped the corporate tax remain in place. Citing the need to improve international competitiveness, America's businesses are clamoring for corporate tax cuts. No matter how much lawmakers may agree, severe budget pressures and reflexive opposition from large swaths of the general public make significant corporate tax reduction a daunting political challenge.

We can't predict the future—especially in today's volatile environment—but all indications are that America is going to have one hell of a debate about the corporate tax over the next few years. This book is a three-part guide to the politics and economics of the corporate tax. Part 1 provides background necessary for an informed debate. Chapter 1 describes the corporate reform proposals now getting the most attention. Chapter 2 is filled with facts and figures about profits and profit taxes—two of the most critical and unpredictable of all economic statistics. Chapter 3 reviews the iron-clad economic arguments for abolition of the corporate tax. Chapter 4 explains how political realities have trumped economics and allowed the corporate tax to survive.

Part 2 of this book highlights the features of the current corporate tax that would be on the table in any reform effort. Chapter 5 discusses the corporate rate that everybody says should be cut. Chapters 6 and 7 describe the major corporate tax breaks that could be on the chopping block in order raise revenue to pay for those rate cuts. Chapters 8 and 9 provide an overview of the increasingly important issue of international taxation. Chapter 10 is about state corporation taxes and their special issues. Corporate tax reform must take into account the mass of small and midsize businesses not subject to corporate tax. Chapter 11 provides a bird's-eye view of "pass-through" businesses, including the fast-growing number of limited liability companies (LLCs) and Subchapter S corporations. Chapter 12 focuses on the complexity of the corporate tax and the efforts (mostly failed) to simplify it.

For many, just making adjustments to the current corporate tax—as President Reagan did in 1986—is not nearly enough. Part 3 steps back from the details and considers the larger picture. Chapter 13 focuses the Flat Tax and the Fair Tax, two proposals for fundamental tax reform that would entirely replace the current income tax with a simplified consumption tax. Chapter 14 explores other major reform options that do not go as far the Flat Tax or the Fair Tax, but would nevertheless entail changes far greater than we experienced in 1986. Now more than ever before, the fate of corporate reform is interwoven with the need for deficit reduction. Chapter 15 concludes the book with a review of the daunting fiscal challenges that America still faces even after the passage of the $2.3 trillion deficit reduction deal—the Budget Control Act of 2011.

CHAPTER 1

Let the Debate Begin

New Pressures for Corporate Tax Reform

Every year, the federal government looks into America's trillion-dollar pot of corporate profits and ladles out a few hundred billion for itself. The basic idea is simple. Government needs money. Corporations have lots of it. For most citizens that feels right. It is an approach to fundraising that has a lot of visceral appeal. The government's tool for this task is the federal tax on corporate profits.

This book is different from most books about corporate tax because it will not ignore ordinary people's perceptions of the tax. This is a democracy and the tax has a strong populist streak. It can stir up a lot of emotion. Our political leaders respond to that emotion. But beyond its basic purpose, the corporate tax has very little to do with human sentiment. It is an undecipherable mass of rules and regulations. It is not user-friendly. It is a three-dimensional chess match between the private and public sector with billions on the line. So while we must use the right side of our brains to understand the politics of the tax, the left side of our brains will be put to work on the mechanics and economics of the tax.

A scandalously large amount of America's brain power is devoted to the corporate tax. You think you've got problems filing your tax return each year. The hassle of the completing Form 1040 is a stroll in the park compared to task facing the typical large corporation. Dozens of employees work year-round to complete a corporate tax return hundreds of pages long. IRS audits routinely run for years. Disputes that end up in court last more than a decade.

When they need outside help, and they often do, corporations do not go to the H&R Block at the local strip mall. They hire high-powered specialists from the nation's leading accounting and law firms. These experts have all the smarts of nuclear physicists. They come with advanced degrees from America's leading universities. And then they spend decades specializing in areas *within* corporate taxation.

The Internal Revenue Service hires the best and brightest as well. They are dedicated professionals of high intellectual caliber. But they are underpaid and generally less experienced than their private-sector counterparts, as the usual career sequence is several years of service at the IRS followed by partnership at a major firm—not the other way around.

In addition to this core of corporate tax professionals who deal with the day-to-day issues of tax practice, there is a legion of equally brainy policy experts. These include law professors, think-tank economists, and the professional tax staff working for Congress and at the Treasury Department. Many make careers studying the current corporate tax and trying to think up ways to make it work better.

It is not all wasted time. The stakes are high. The corporate tax plays a critical role in the economy. Most of the tax is paid by large, publicly held companies. These corporations account for the bulk of the nation's research and its exports. U.S. multinational corporations are on the front lines of the battle for international competitiveness. Other countries around the world are boldly reforming their corporate taxes hoping to give their businesses an edge in an increasingly global marketplace. Is America going to be left behind?

Yes, the corporate tax is full of intellectual challenges that make even the experts' minds swim. But for better or worse, our nation's tax laws are made by politicians who ultimately care little about academic views. On small changes in corporate tax law—the "rifle shots" and "tax earmarks" that can be kept out of the public spotlight—corporate lobbyists and self-interested contributors are lawmakers' primary influence. When big changes in the corporate tax are under consideration, lawmakers must answer to public opinion. And public opinion on the corporate tax is often anything but rational.

The Old Debate

The most natural thing in American politics is the framing of issues as a battle between conservative Republicans and liberal Democrats. On the cable news channels, policy issues are routinely presented as debates between the two major parties. It is easy to dismiss the time-compressed sound-bite discussion as shallow. But even still, underlying all the sloganeering, there are usually fairly respectable intellectual arguments behind both political points of view.

As Washington policy debates go, the debate about corporate tax reform is an unusual animal. Sure, there is the usual conservative/liberal divide. Republicans hate the tax and would love to see it disappear. Democrats could not imagine the world without a corporate tax. But when it comes to the intellectual underpinnings, the debate is entirely one-sided: *There is no good economic argument for the corporation tax.* If you want to defend the corporate tax, you should to steer clear of economics. The conservatives hold the economic high ground.

In a nutshell the economic case against the corporate tax is simply this: corporate profits are already taxed at the individual level. Profits that are distributed to shareholders are taxed as dividends. Profits that are retained by the corporation are taxed as capital gains when the stock is sold. A tax at the corporate level on those profits adds a second layer of tax.

Economic efficiency requires equal taxation of all income (except in special cases, such as with pollution, when activities impose uncompensated cost on the economy or, as with industrial research, when activities bestow uncompensated benefits). In other words, taxes as a percentage of profits should be equal. The political implication of this economic logic is that the corporate tax should be repealed so that some business profits are not double-taxed while others are only taxed once. Short of repeal, the corporate tax should be made as small as possible. Sure, a lot of folks deeply distrust and dislike corporations, but that is not a economic rationale for imposing a separate major tax on them.

So why, if the economic case is so iron-clad, is corporate tax still thriving in the 21st century? The answer is that supporters of the tax have something much better than academic arguments. The near complete lack of intellectual backing for the Democratic view that taxing corporate profits is justified is more than offset by the tax's strong emotional appeal. Most individuals reject the conclusion that corporations should not be subject to tax. If you doubt this, next time you are at a party, try floating the view that in order to get the economy moving, the Exxon-Mobil tax bill must be reduced to zero from now until the end of time.

Instinctively, Republican politicians know that repealing the corporate tax is a non-starter no matter how many professors come out of the woodwork to back them up. There is no advantage for them in trying to educate the public in economics. So, even though they are fully convinced by the intellectual case for repeal, and in their heart of hearts they wish it could be done, they won't waste political capital by publicly airing their real views.

New Challenges

The United States had a corporation tax as early as 1909, three years before the 16th amendment cleared the path for the income tax Throughout its 100-plus-year history, conservatives have based their arguments against the corporate tax on mainstream economics. They argue that the corporate tax sets off a chain reaction of unfavorable economic events. It goes like this. The corporate tax lowers the rate of return on business investment. This reduces capital formation. With less capital, there are fewer jobs, and those workers with jobs are less productive with less capital, so they earn lower wages. The U.S. standard of living drops and U.S. competitiveness suffers.

The liberal case has always been based on fairness. The political left argues that is morally unacceptable that powerful corporations earning enormous sums should not contribute their "fair share" to the public welfare. Moreover, the owners of corporations—the shareholders—are mostly from upper-income households. According to the liberal view, a fair tax system is a progressive tax system—a system where not only tax payments, but also tax rates, rise with income. The corporation tax is an essential component of any tax system that claims to be fair and progressive.

Recent developments have added new fuel to both sides of the debate. Over the last decade, governments around the world have dramatically reduced their corporate tax rates. In the United States, when state corporate taxes are added on to the 35 percent federal rate, the average corporate tax rate is 39.2 percent. The average corporate rate of other member nations of the Organization of Economic Cooperation and Development (OECD) is 25 percent.[1]

---

[1] Organization for Economic Cooperation and Development, OECD Tax Database, Corporate and Capital Income Taxes, Table II.1, "Basic (non-targeted) Corporate Income Tax Rates, 2011, http://www.oecd.org/dataoecd/26/56/33717459.xls.

And all indications are that foreign rates will continue to fall. In Canada, a recent conservative election victory makes it likely the government will achieve its goal of a combined federal-provincial tax rate of 25 percent in 2012. In the United Kingdom, the government plans to reduce its corporate tax rate by one percentage point a year until it reaches 24 percent in 2014. Japan planned to lower its corporate tax rate from 39.4 to 35 percent in April 2011, but the earthquake in the preceding month put these plans on hold. These changes leave the United States, which in the late 1980s had one of the lowest corporate tax rates, with the second highest corporate tax rate in the world. If, as seems likely, the Japanese government fulfills its intention to lower its corporate rate, the United States will have the dubious distinction of having the highest corporate tax rate in the world.

Lowering the corporate tax rate has always been desirable tax policy, as I shall discuss in Chapter 5. Developments around the world are turning it into a necessity. But there is tremendous pressure working against rate reduction. It is commonplace these days to hear politicians say we need to reduce the corporate tax rate to 25 percent. Such a 10-percentage-point decline would reduce federal revenue by approximately $100 billion annually.

Where is money like this to come from when the future of federal finance has never looked bleaker? At the end of 2011, U.S. government debt held by the public will equal approximately 69 percent of GDP, its highest level since World War II. But there really is no precedent in American history for our situation. Because of our aging population and the skyrocketing cost of government-subsidized health care, there is no end in sight for the growth of the national debt. It is purely a matter of arithmetic: without large and painful spending cuts or tax hikes (or a combination of the two), the government of the United States is on the path to fiscal collapse.

Another economic development that poses a major political obstacle to corporate tax reform is the increasing gap between America's rich and poor. Yes, we are talking about that unpleasant topic known as "class warfare." As with everything in economics, there is dispute about the exact numbers. But figures from the non-partisan Congressional Budget Office (CBO) illustrate the point. In 1979, the after-tax income of the richest 1 percent of Americans accounted for 7.5 percent of the national total. By 2007, the share for that group had more than doubled to 17.1 percent. Over the same period the income share of the bottom 40 percent of the population dropped from 19.1 to 14.2 percent.

Although economists are unsure about whether the burden of the corporate tax is borne by shareholders or is passed to workers in the form of lower wages, the public generally perceives the corporate tax as a tax on the corporate fat cats and trust fund babies. To the extent this view prevails, cutting corporate taxes will be seen as contributing to economic inequality.

So there are new and powerful forces pulling corporate tax reform in polar opposite directions. Democrats—even those sympathetic to business—argue that unprecedented budget pressure means we simply cannot afford corporate tax relief and that widening income disparity makes it morally objectionable. Republicans—even those focused on deficit reduction—argue that unprecedented international competition means we simply cannot afford not to cut the corporate tax.

Proposals for Change

In recent years, there have been a number of high-profile challenges to the corporate tax status quo. Some are part of efforts at overall tax reform. Some are part of ambitious deficit reduction plans. All share a common theme: the need to improve America's competitiveness by reducing the 35 percent corporate tax rate. All propose to reduce corporate tax breaks to pay for the rate reduction. Most, but not all, of these plans are extremely vague about what specific corporate tax breaks should be trimmed back. Here's a rundown of some of the proposals.

President Obama's 2011 State of the Union Address

Tax reform requires presidential leadership. So among the efforts and proposals out there, President Obama's is the most important. On several occasions, the president has voiced strong support for corporate tax reform. The most prominent of these mentions was his State of the Union Address on January 25, 2011, where he said

> Over the years, a parade of lobbyists has rigged the tax code to benefit particular companies and industries. Those with accountants or lawyers to work the system can end up paying no taxes at all. But all the rest are hit with one of the highest corporate tax rates in the world. It makes no sense, and it has to change. So tonight, I'm asking Democrats and Republicans to simplify the system. Get rid of the loopholes. Level the playing field. And use the savings to lower the corporate tax rate for the first time in 25 years—without adding to our deficit.

All of Washington knows the Treasury Department is hard at work on developing and analyzing specific proposals that would meet the president's goals. The Treasury tax policy staff has met numerous times with congressional staff, stakeholders ranging from CFOs of *Fortune* 500 companies to small-business trade associations, academics, and other experts to discuss a wide range of ideas. Although there have been rumors that the Treasury has been looking at plan that would reduce the corporate rate to 26 percent, no proposal has been released.

House Budget Resolution for Fiscal Year 2012 (the "Ryan Plan")

Many members of Congress also have expressed strong support for lowering the corporate tax rate. The most important of these pronouncements comes from Speaker of the House John Boehner (R-Ohio), who in May of 2011 said

> If we want to put Americans back to work, I think lowering the tax rate is critically important. To do that, I think we have to look at tax expenditures, deductions, credits, and other gimmicks embedded in the tax code.

Similarly, in March of 2011, the chief tax writer in the House of Representatives, Ways and Means Committee Chairman Dave Camp (R-Michigan), told the *Wall Street Journal* he would like to reduce the corporate and individual rates to 25 percent and pay for these rate cuts with the elimination of deductions and credits.

Republican sentiments about the corporation tax became more formal (although not much more specific) when the House of Representatives adopted its budget resolution. On April 15, the U.S. House of Representatives passed its budget resolution, developed by Budget Committee Chairman Paul Ryan (R-Wisconsin). The Ryan plan, entitled "A Path to Prosperity," attempts to put the nation's finances on a sustainable path without raising taxes. The plan is most famous for its controversial cuts in Medicare benefits.

Less well known is its tax reform component. The description of the plan explains that under current law, "the biggest corporations that can afford the best lawyers have figured out how to use the code to avoid paying taxes altogether." To remedy the problem, the House budget would cut the top individual and the corporate rates from 35 to 25 percent and pay for these rate cuts with unspecified cuts in "loopholes and special carve-outs."

Of course the ideas of President Obama and the Republican leadership are hardly revolutionary. They are just following the golden rule of tax reform: *lower the rates and broaden the base.* This was the approach adopted by the Reagan administration when it began its tax reform efforts in 1984, and by the entire Congress when it lowered the corporate tax rate from 46 to 34 percent in the Tax Reform Act of 1986.

The following sections provide a quick summary of other recent proposals for corporate tax reform.

President Bush's 2005 Tax Reform Panel

In November 2005, President George W. Bush's Advisory Panel on Federal Tax Reform proposed a Simplified Income Tax plan that would lower the rate and broaden the base of both the individual and corporate taxes without either raising or reducing the revenue collected by each. On the corporate side, the rate reduction from 35 to 31.5 percent is paid for by eliminating special deductions and credits by ending the practice of allowing large publicly traded partnerships to escape corporation tax. On the individual side, the component of the plan with particular relevance here is the exclusion from taxable income of 100 percent of corporate dividends and of 75 percent of the capital gain on sales of corporate stock. The panel also recommended that the United States exempt foreign profits of U.S. corporations from U.S. tax.

The 2007 Treasury Study

As part of its study of the effect of tax rules on competitiveness, the Treasury Department in 2007 presented estimates indicating that if all major corporate tax breaks were eliminated—including accelerated depreciation for equipment—the corporate tax rate could be reduced to 28 percent without reducing revenue. If accelerated depreciation of equipment is retained, the corporate tax rate could be reduced to 31 percent.

The 2007 Rangel Tax Reform Plan

In October of 2007, Charles Rangel (D-New York), then-chairman of the House Ways and Means Committee, introduced a bill he described as "the mother of all tax reform plans." The corporate component of the Rangel plan would reduce the corporate tax rate to 30.5 percent and pay for the rate reduction with a repeal of the incentive for domestic manufacturing and a tightening of the tax rules on foreign profits. On the individual side, the plan would increase taxes on households with incomes above $200,000 and use the revenue to repeal the individual alternative minimum tax, the burden of which falls primarily on upper-middle-income households.

The Wyden-Coates Tax Reform Plan

In 2010, Democrat Senator Ron Wyden of Oregon and Republican Senator Judd Gregg of New Hampshire introduced the "Bipartisan Tax Fairness and Simplification Act." The proposed legislation combines individual and corporate tax reform. On the individual side, the bill keeps the top individual rates, now scheduled to increase to 39.6 percent in 2013, at 35 percent; it reduces the number of other rates from five to three; and it triples the standard deduction. It partially offsets these cuts with higher taxes on fringe benefits and cuts in some other tax benefits. On the corporate side, the tax rate is cut a whopping 11 percent, from 35 to 24 percent. The revenue lost from this rate cuts is partially offset with a significant increase in tax on foreign profits, less generous write-offs for purchases of capital equipment, and a partial reduction in the deduction for interest payments. Senator Gregg did not seek reelection in 2010. Since his retirement, Senator Wyden has reintroduced the legislation with Republican Senator Dan Coates of Indiana as his cosponsor.

The Bowles-Simpson Deficit Reduction Plan

In December 2010, the National Commission on Fiscal Responsibility and Reform, chaired by former White House chief of staff Erskine Bowles (a Democrat) and former senator Alan Simpson (a Republican), issued a report with its recommendations for deficit reduction, including spending cuts, tax increases, and tax reforms. The report recommended the corporate tax be set between 23 and 29 percent. The report's "illustrative plan" would reduce the rate to 28 percent, eliminate all deductions and credits, and modify the U.S. corporate tax so that foreign profits were completely exempt from U.S. tax.

Illusion of Consensus

With so many proposals out there using the same basic rate-cutting, base-broadening template, you might draw the conclusion that corporate tax reform is one of the easier problems for Washington to solve. While fierce partisanship is the norm for our recent debates on fiscal policy, could corporate tax reform be the "low-hanging fruit"? After all, the current White House and Republican leaders seem to be in agreement on this one.

But any notion of a developing consensus is an illusion. There are irreconcilable differences about the most fundamental aspect of the exercise: the revenue impact of corporate tax reform. Business groups and conservatives can go along with some paring down of tax breaks, but overall corporate tax reform must be a corporate tax cut. Liberals can go along with some rate cuts, but overall they want tax reform that still helps reduce the deficit. Revenue-neutral reform, as proposed by the president, seems like a reasonable compromise. But it is not at all clear either side would agree to such a change that leaves out their prime goal. Once we get beyond the niceties of supporting tax reform in concept, the usual debilitating partisan bickering will gridlock corporate tax reform just like any other budget issue.

And there is another reason to be pessimistic about prospects. Right now, most of the talk from politicians is about rate cuts and getting rid of big, bad loopholes. That's the stuff the people like to hear. But if it is ever really going to happen, corporate tax reform must include a frank and detailed discussion about cuts in specific deductions and credits. That will instantly deflate support for reform. Once it is revealed whose tax breaks are on the chopping block, the public will be deluged with messages informing them that the tax breaks in question are essential to keeping jobs in America. Lobbyists will swarm the hallways of Capitol Hill telling legislators how proposed changes will kill jobs in their districts. The vested interests will mount all-out campaigns that will turn tax reform lions into political mice.

"As long as tax reform is offered in the abstract, everyone rallies to the cause," senior Ways and Means Committee member and Democrat Richard Neal said recently. "When it becomes specific, people start to fall off."[2]

None of the proposals outlined here has any chance of becoming law soon. But reform is desperately needed. To understand why, and what the realistic prospects are for change, are the subjects of the rest of this book.

Summary

Corporate tax reform is now getting a lot of extra attention from our nation's leaders, who want to improve America's competitiveness. But tight budgets and the public's innate dislike of corporate tax cuts pose significant obstacles.

---

[2] John D. McKinnon, "Tax Plan Aims for 25% Cap," *Wall Street Journal*, March 17, 2011.

Profits and Profit Tax, by the Numbers

Volatile, Unstable, and Closely Watched

It is often said that the corporate tax is on the way out. How can it possibly survive? It is obsolete. Great leaps forward in globalization and financial innovation have made it difficult to justify and impossible to collect. Well, somebody ought to tell the folks over at the Treasury Department. Over the next decade the federal government plans to collect over $400 billion a year in corporation tax—about 10 percent of total federal revenue.

Up until now, the previous record for annual corporate tax receipts was the $370 billion collected in 2007. This was an unexpected windfall for the Treasury. In 2004 Treasury economists were projecting that corporate tax revenue in 2007 would be only $230 billion.

A few years later the exact opposite occurred. Treasury revenues were coming in way below projections. In 2008 the Treasury estimated that corporate revenues would remain comfortably above $300 billion every year in the foreseeable future. But then the bottom dropped out of the economy. In 2009 the IRS only took in $138 billion—a decline of almost two-thirds from the 2007 level.

Economists' forecasts are always off. (If they could really predict the future, they would not be economists but billionaire investors.) But of all the uncertainty in the future, one of the most uncertain things is the level of corporate tax revenue.

The Profit Roller Coaster

The main problem with forecasting corporate tax revenue is that the corporate tax is a tax on profits. All economic data moves up and down with the business cycle, but profit movements are more erratic than most. Over the last 15 years it has been a roller-coaster ride, as you can see for yourself in Figure 2-1. After hitting a 30-year high in the late 1990s, profits dipped to 7.6 percent of GDP during the 2001 recession, only to achieve a new record high of 12.0 percent of GDP in 2006. The latest recession caused profits to decline again to 8.8 percent of GDP. But since then they have rebounded strongly again.

Figure 2-1. Profits as a percentage of GDP, 1955–2010. Shaded areas are recession years. Source: U.S. Department of Commerce, Bureau of Economic Analysis.

Profits—like salaries, benefits, interest, and self-employment income—are part of national income. As shown in Figure 2-1, there is no such thing as a typical year when we talk about profits. Because any snapshot can be misleading, Figure 2-2 uses averages over time to compare profits to other economic data. Over the 12-year period from 1999 to 2010, corporate profits on average were 12.1 percent of national income. Non-corporate income—which includes income from the self-employed, income from partnerships, and farm income—also equaled 12.1 percent of national income. At 69.7 percent, employee compensation—including wages, salaries, and employee benefits—is by far the largest component of national income. Net interest, at 6.2 percent of national income, makes up the remainder.

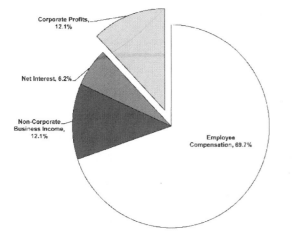

Figure 2-2. Shares of national income, 1999–2010 average. Source: U.S. Department of Commerce, Bureau of Economic Analysis.

Don't let the relatively small size of profits in overall national income fool you. Profits play a huge role in the economy. Profits are the lifeblood of our capitalist system. They send signals to investors about where to put their capital. Where profits are, capital is sure to follow. And when profits dry up, capital gets scarce. The wonder of free-market capitalism is that by following their self-interest, investors are maximizing growth of the entire economy. The market is always trying to direct capital to its most productive uses. This is Adam Smith's famous "invisible hand" at work. Of course, government intervenes in all aspects of the economy through taxation and regulation—often skewing capital away from its most efficient uses. But that does not change the importance of profits as *the* device for signaling to the private sector where, when, and how much investment should take place.

Revenue You Can't Count On

As volatile as corporate profits are, government receipts from the tax on corporate profits are even more volatile, as shown in Figure 2-3. For example, between 2006 and 2009, corporate tax receipts as a percentage of GDP dropped from 2.7 to 1.0 percent. Expressed as a percentage of total federal tax receipts, corporate tax receipts over this period dropped from 14.7 to 6.6 percent. As with corporate profits, there is no such thing as a typical year for corporate tax receipts.

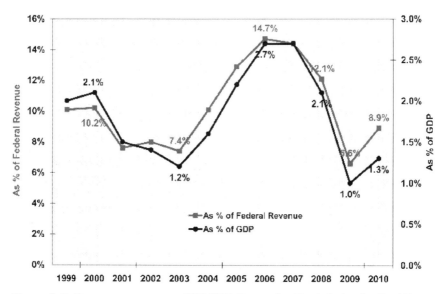

Figure 2-3. Corporate tax revenue, 1999–2010. Source: President's Budget for Fiscal Year 2012.

Figure 2-4 shows the composition of federal tax receipts on average over the 1999–2010 period. The largest revenue source is the individual income tax, accounting for 45.2 percent of total federal revenue. Payroll taxes for the Social Security and Medicare trust funds are 36.6 percent of revenues. The corporate tax takes the bronze—a distant third place in the contest for largest revenue source. Over the 1999–2010 period it accounted for 10.5 percent of federal revenue.

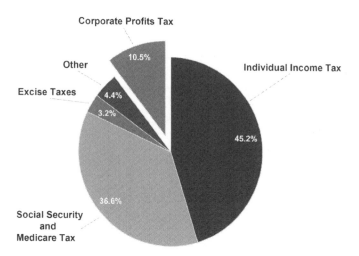

Figure 2-4. The composition of federal revenue, 1999–2010 average. Source: President's Budget for Fiscal Year 2012.

Economists divide data movements over time into two: short-term cycles and long-term trends. Figure 2-3 showed you that short-term cyclicality of corporate tax revenue is very pronounced. The long-term trend is shown in Figure 2-5. Between 1955 and 1980 there was a marked decline in corporate tax revenue. After the Korean War (1950–1953) corporate tax revenue averaged about 4.4 percent of GDP. In the 1960s it averaged about 3.8 percent of GDP. And in the 1980s the average dropped to 2.7 percent of GDP. Since the 1980s—although it is subject to significant movements—the average has hovered slightly below 2 percent of GDP for three decades.

Figure 2-5. Corporate tax receipts as a percentage of GDP, 1955–2010. President's Budget for Fiscal Year 2012.

Much of the decline is attributable to the decline in the corporate tax rate. This is shown in Figure 2-6. During the Vietnam War, the rate had been as high as 52.8 percent. It was reduced to 46 percent in 1979, and the Tax Reform Act of 1986 rocked the corporate world with a rate reduction from 46 to 34 percent. As part of his deficit reduction program in 1993, President Clinton proposed increasing the corporate rate from 34 to 36 percent. Ultimately Congress settled on a 35 percent rate, and that's where it still stands today.

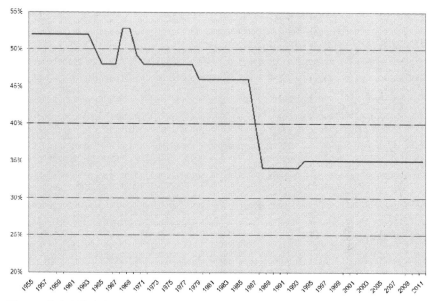

Figure 2-6. U.S. federal corporate tax rate, 1955–2011. Source: Tax Foundation.

But reduction in corporate tax rate is only part of the story of the decline in corporate tax revenues. There is also a lot of corporate revenue being lost to the erosion of the tax base. Part of this is due to Congress enacting more tax breaks (discussed in Chapters 6 and 7). Part is due to the shifting of profits outside the United States to low-tax jurisdictions (discussed in Chapter 9). And part is due to the rapid increase in use of untaxed organizational forms by small and medium-size businesses (see Chapter 10).

Two Sets of Books

There are as many ways to measure profits as Baskin-Robbins has flavors of ice cream. In this book, readers will be spared most of the excruciating details, but understanding some of the more important differences in profit measures is essential for the savvy follower of the corporate tax scene. The three most important measures of profits are *economic* profits, *book* profits (also commonly referred to as *accounting* profits), and *taxable* profits.

The numbers reported earlier in Figures 2-1 and 2-2 are economic profits tabulated at the Department of Commerce. Economic profits are important components of the National Income and Product Accounts, the official economic statistics of the U.S. government. These numbers are computed by economists to help other economists assess the health of the economy. The quarterly release on economic profits is anxiously anticipated by everybody trying to gauge the strength of the economy. Individual corporations and their accountants do not bother computing economic profits.

Publicly traded corporations report their book profits to shareholders every quarter. To compute book profits, corporate accountants generally follow the rules promulgated by the Financial Accounting Standards Board (FASB). These rules can be mind-numbingly complex. Entire books are written on arcane subjects like accounting for inventories. And, because so much is on the line, formulation of the rules is often the subject of heated debate. For example, the high-tech community in Silicon Valley went ballistic when FASB proposed and then succeeded in changing accounting rules so that the exercise of stock options was an expense deducted from profits reported to shareholders.

Like economic profits, book profits get widespread coverage in the financial press, and corporations take great pains in calculating book profits. The quarterly releases of each company's book profits are important to Wall Street analysts looking for clues about a company's prospects. If earnings-per-share beat market expectations, a stock price will usually rise. And if earnings-per-share "disappoint" the markets, share prices will fall. The "earnings" in those earnings-per-share figures are after-tax book profits. To bolster stock prices—and their own compensation—corporate executives want book profits to be as large as possible.

Besides book profits, the other measure of profits that directly concerns business is taxable profit. This is the amount of profit reported to the IRS. It is the amount subject to the 35 percent corporate tax rate. To minimize Uncle Sam's share of the take, corporate managers want this number as small as possible. Yes, corporations keep two sets of books and, yes, it is all perfectly legal.

The rules for computing taxable profits are found in the Internal Revenue Code—a compilation of tax statutes written by Congress—and in the tax regulations written by the IRS and the Treasury Department. These rules for taxable profits can be very different from FASB rules for book profits. For example, because Congress wants to provide an incentive for the purchase of capital equipment, it allows the purchase price of capital equipment to be written off more quickly than FASB allows. In other words, *tax* depreciation is faster than *book* depreciation. This generally results in tax profits being smaller than book profits.

Another example will illustrate the difference working in the opposite direction. Corporations will often charge additions to pension reserve as expenses that reduce book profits. But the IRS does not allow deductions for additions to these reserves. This rule results in tax profits being larger than reported book profits.

These examples are only two of many. The important thing to remember is that book profits and taxable profits can be very different. And so it is entirely possible for a corporation to report strong earnings to shareholders and pay zero corporate taxes to Uncle Sam. This phenomenon usually provokes outrage from the general public, and it is what motivates Congress to impose a minimum tax on corporations where the tax base more closely resembles book profits. Unfortunately, the current corporate minimum tax adds considerable complexity to the tax law and does little to eliminate the specter of tax-free high-profit corporations.

A Tax on Big Business

Individuals file Form 1040 annually with the IRS. Corporations file Form 1120. For tax year 2008—the latest year data is currently available—nearly 6.3 million corporations filed a Form 1120 with the IRS. The vast majority of these returns were not subject to corporate tax. Some—about 800,000—were just inactive shell corporations. The majority—about 4 million—were entirely excused from corporate tax because they met the requirements of Subchapter S of the Internal Revenue Code. (We'll talk more about Subchapter S corporations in Chapter 10).

That left about 1.9 million corporations potentially subject to corporate tax. In tax lingo these are called Subchapter C corporations. Among Subchapter C corporations, the distribution of the corporate tax burden is heavily skewed toward a comparatively small number of these large corporations. This is shown in Figure 2-7. In 2008, the 1,911 largest C corporations—those with over $250 million in sales—constituted only 0.1 percent of the total number of C corporations, but they paid 83 percent of all corporate tax. Figure 2-7 illustrates one of the most salient facts about the corporate tax: *the corporate tax is primarily a tax on America's largest businesses.*

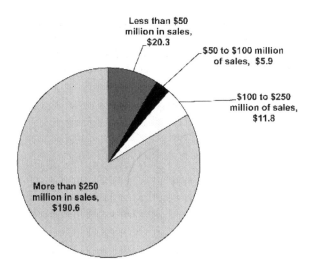

Figure 2-7. Corporate tax revenue, 2008, by size of corporation (tax revenues in billions of dollars). Source: Internal Revenue Service.

There are exceptions to this rule. There are small businesses that are organized as C corporations. And there are large businesses that have been able to avoid C corporation status. But for the most part the corporate tax is paid by large corporations whose stock is traded on the New York Stock Exchange and the NASDAQ.

The Bottom Line

Wall Street is obsessed with profits. That means corporate executives must also be obsessed with profits. Book profits reported to shareholders are after-tax profits. That means the tax on corporate profits is a major concern for CEOs and has a major impact on stock prices. For the financial press and the titans of Wall Street, corporate tax may not be the sexiest topic, but it is always there, lurking, with the potential to either deflate or boost share prices.

The corporate tax got a lot of attention from the markets in the 1980s when a leveraged buyout boom had Wall Street buzzing with big deals. The most famous of these was the debt-financed purchase of RJR Nabisco, subsequently documented in the best-selling book and movie *Barbarians at the Gate*. In a typical leveraged buyout, a group of investors with a relatively small amount of equity would issue enormous amounts of "junk bonds" to finance acquisition of a target company. Besides bringing fresh perspective and new expertise to acquired business, value was also created by the replacement of equity with debt. The new deductions for all the additional interest expense could significantly reduce the acquired corporation's tax liability.

In Washington there was much concern that this use of debt could undermine financial stability. Congress gave serious consideration to proposals limiting the deductibility of interest on junk bonds. But then in 1987 stock prices collapsed by more than 20 percent in a single day. Some experts blamed the crash on Congress's tough talk about limiting tax benefits. Congress backed off. And in the end it adopted only the most modest restrictions on the deductibility of interest. In subsequent years, the leveraged buyout craze settled down pretty much on its own, but the use of leverage to reduce taxes remains a major factor in corporate finance.

These days Wall Street's main concern with the corporate tax is its impact on each corporation's *effective tax rate*. If a corporation can permanently reduce its effective tax rate, for example, from 35 to 28 percent, this will result in a permanent increase in after-tax profits of about 10 percent. Stock prices are a function in part of expected future after-tax profits, and generally a 10 percent increase in expected future profits will increase a stock price by a similar order of magnitude.

Just as corporate CEOs are evaluated on reported after-tax profits, corporate tax managers are evaluated on reported effective tax rates. Observers of the tax scene have frequently commented that since the 1990s, the character of corporate tax departments has changed from that of a cost center to a profit center. The job of corporate tax departments is no longer to merely comply with tax laws but to contribute to the bottom line. Many attribute this change in attitude to the rise in the use of corporate tax shelters in the 1990s and increasing propensity of corporations to locate valuable intellectual property (like patents and trademarks) in tax havens.

For many business executives and Wall Street investors, the effective tax rate is a lens through which they view the corporate tax. Because of its central importance, it is useful to understand how an effective tax rate is calculated. Basically, it is a ratio with tax expense in the numerator and before-tax profit in the denominator. Now here is the strange part. The tax expense in the numerator is not what the corporation pays to the IRS and other tax authorities. It is what FASB rules deem to be the proper accrual of tax expense.

Actual tax payments and FASB tax expense can be very different numbers. For example, as noted earlier, actual taxes are reduced when Congress permits more accelerated depreciation, but reported tax expense is not reduced. On the other hand, in many circumstances, reported income tax expense does closely track actual cash payments. For example, in the common situation where a corporation shifts profits from a high-tax to a low-tax country, there is a reduction in both booked tax expense (the numerators of the effective tax rate) and in actual taxes paid.

The potential duality of tax expense and actual taxes paid means that corporations must consider the impact of tax planning on both measures. Not only that, it is widely believed that corporations are more concerned about lowering their reported effective tax rate than their actual tax bills.

Actual tax expense paid to the IRS is confidential taxpayer information that is not publicly available. Except in rare cases—as when there is tax dispute that goes to court or a voluntarily disclosure by the corporation—information about actual tax payments paid by any single corporation is unknown to the public (and even to most of the government outside the IRS). The IRS only discloses aggregate information on tax payments.

Falling Effective Tax Rates

One of the more notable developments in corporate finance in recent years has been the significant decline in effective tax rates reported to shareholders. This has occurred despite the fact that the statutory corporate tax has remained at 35 percent over the entire period.

Table 2-1 lists the 20 U.S. corporations with the largest book profits in 2007. It then compares the average reported effective tax rate for 1997–1999 with the average effective tax rate for 2005–2007. Clearly the trend over this period is toward lower effective tax rates. Of the 19 firms for whom the comparison can be made, 18 had lower effective tax rates. For these corporations, the average decline was 5.5 percentage points.

This decline in effective tax rates has little to do with Congress enacting more tax breaks. It primarily is attributable to U.S. corporations doing more business outside the United States, a steady decline in foreign tax rates, and the increasing ability of tax managers to shift a disproportionate share of profits to tax havens like Ireland, Switzerland, Bermuda, and the Cayman Islands.

Table 2-1. The declining effective tax rates of America's most profitable corporations

Corporation	Book Profits (Billions)	Reported Effective Tax Rate		
		1997–1999 Average	2005–2007 Average	Change
Altria	$9.8	40.3%	29.6%	−10.7%
AT&T	$12.0	37.7%	27.7%	−10.0%
Bank of America	$15.0	36.4%	31.7%	−4.7%
Berkshire Hathaway	$13.2	33.4%	32.7%	−0.7%
Chevron	$18.7	47.6%	44.1%	−3.5%
Cisco Systems	$7.3	40.9%	26.0%	−14.9%
ConocoPhillips	$11.9	47.3%	45.4%	−1.9%
Exxon Mobil	$40.6	36.1%	42.7%	+6.6%
General Electric	$22.2	29.6%	16.8%	−12.8%
Goldman Sachs	$11.6	n/a	33.5%	--
Hewlett-Packard	$7.3	27.7%	22.3%	−5.4%
IBM	$10.4	32.3%	30.7%	−1.6%
Intel	$7.0	34.3%	27.9%	−6.4%
JPMorgan Chase	$15.4	36.2%	31.4%	−4.8%
Johnson & Johnson	$10.6	27.9%	22.6%	−5.3%
Microsoft	$14.1	35.6%	29.0%	−6.6%
Pfizer	$8.1	26.6%	18.6%	−8.0%
Procter & Gamble	$10.3	34.7%	30.1%	−4.6%
Wal-Mart Stores	$12.7	35.7%	33.6%	−2.1%
Wells Fargo	$8.1	39.4%	32.6%	−6.8%
Group average*		**35.8%**	**30.3%**	**−5.5%**

* Excluding Goldman Sachs, which was not a publicly traded company in the 1990s

Source: Company annual reports

Summary

The volatility of corporate profits is a source of fascination to economists and a constant headache for policymakers. Most corporate tax is paid by publicly traded corporations. Their effective tax rates, tracked closely by corporate executives and Wall Street analysts, have been trending downward.

CHAPTER 3

The Overwhelming Case Against the Corporate Tax

A Drag on Productivity and Competitiveness

For a book that is supposed to provide objective analysis, the title of this chapter may seem a little overbearing. After all, aren't there two sides to every story? Well, when it comes to the *economics* of corporate tax, the answer is a big fat *no*. There is no economic justification for its existence. This statement boils the blood of liberals, and it surprises most of the general public. Sorry to hurt people's feelings, but there is no escaping the truth. And this is the almost universally accepted view among economists, both Republican and Democrat. In fact, of all the bad taxes out there, economists consider the corporate tax the most harmful to economic growth.

If the corporate tax must exist, of course we should strive to make it as efficient and simple as possible. And much of Part 2 of this book discusses the possibilities along these lines. But we must always keep in the back of our minds that all we are doing is making a fundamentally flawed situation less awful—like when we order a Diet Coke with our double cheeseburger.

Why are economists so whiny about the corporate tax? Are they so enamored with free-market capitalism that they are willing to let the world's most powerful and rich organizations shirk the responsibility of contributing to the national welfare? Economists *are* devoted to minimizing government interference in the marketplace. They want the government to stay clear of market decision-making. They want a level playing field. In the realm of business taxation, this veneration of the free market translates into the commandment, *Thou shalt tax all business income equally*. That means all business income should be taxed once. The corporate tax double-taxes business profits.

When economists condemn the corporate tax, they are not thinking about politics or even about popular conceptions of fairness. They are focused on long-term economic growth. Their models tell them the corporate tax is a drag on national productivity. There are two reasons for this. First, the corporate tax shrinks the size of the nation's capital stock. And second, because it alters the allocation of capital, the efficiency of the capital stock is diminished. Besides—and here's the main point—corporate profits are already taxed at the individual level.

To illustrate their concerns, let's suppose we lived on island that had only two kinds of businesses: apple growing and peach growing. Now suppose all production is subject to tax. But also, for some reason that no one can remember, apple production is subject to a second tax. The second layer of tax on apples has two effects. First, the tax reduces the overall profitability of the fruit business. Overall investment in the island's economy declines.

The second problem with the additional tax on apples is that it shifts the mix of the production away from apples to peaches. If there were no second tax on apples, the allocation of resources between apple and peach production would be determined purely by efficiency considerations. Besides making island production smaller, the tax-induced switch from apples to peaches makes the mix of production less efficient. If government must have the revenue, it would be better to tax apple and peach production equally, or even better from the economists' perspective, tax the *consumption* of fruit instead of its production.

The corporate tax is analogous to our hypothetical second tax on apples. It not only reduces the capital stock, but it leaves us with a mix of capital that is less productive.

The Double-Tax Burden

Corporate profits are subject to tax at the corporate level and at the individual level. Here's is the simplest case. Suppose a corporation earns $100 of profit. With a 35 percent tax rate, it pays $35 of corporation tax. If all the remaining $65 of profit is distributed to shareholders, those dividends are subject to income tax at a 15 percent rate—an additional $9.75 of tax. So, total tax from the underlying $100 of income is $45.75 (that is, $35 plus $9.75). The combined tax rate on this profit is approximately 46 percent. That compares with other income taxed at the top individual rate of 35 percent, and with capital gains from non-corporate investment, free of any corporate tax, which are only subject to a 15 percent capital gains rate.

There are many twists and turns in reality that make quantifying the double tax on corporate profits more complicated than this example. For one thing, each layer of the double tax is far from the textbook ideal. Both the corporate and individual taxes are leaky buckets. On the corporate level, many businesses get tax breaks that lower their tax bill below 35 percent of profits. At an individual level, many shareholders—namely pension funds, university endowments, and some lucky foreigners—pay no individual taxes. Taken together, these leakages can reduce the combined corporate and individual tax burden on corporate profits considerably below the 46 percent rate calculated above.

Then there is the matter that our tax rules are constantly changing and uncertain. In the late 1990s, dividends got no special treatment and the top individual rate was 39.6 percent. That means the combined individual and corporate tax burden was almost 60 percent. Looking to the future, both the current 35 percent top individual rate and the 15 percent dividends rate are scheduled to expire at the end of 2012. Congress will probably not let tax rates revert all the way to pre-2000 levels, but nothing in this political and economic environment is certain.

These are important details. But the basic problem of double taxation of corporate profits cannot be obscured: large amounts of corporate profits are generally subject to double tax while most other forms of investment income generally are subject to a single layer of tax. In the real world, taxes are messy. But the corporate tax makes a mess like no other. The existence of the corporate tax means we have *a whole tax system* taxing profits on top of another tax system that already taxes those profits.

The double taxation of corporate profits sets in motion a series of bad economic behaviors. By "bad" we mean "inefficient," in the sense that these behaviors are different from what would occur in a market without distortions. The bad economic outcomes resulting from the double taxation of corporate profits fall into four categories. First, there is the overall reduction in business investment due to the tax. Second, there is shift in investment away from the double-taxed corporate sector. Third, there is shift from equity to debt financing. Fourth, there is shift away from dividends and toward retained earnings. The first distortion makes the capital stock smaller. The last three distortions make the capital stock less efficient.

Problem 1: Less Capital Formation

To improve long-term economic growth and competitiveness, it is essential to increase capital formation. The stock of *tangible* capital is increased by investment in plants and equipment. The stock of *intangible* capital is built up by investment in research that develops new technology. Without physical capital and without new technology, U.S. workers do not have the tools to maintain their high level of productivity and competitiveness. Because wage growth depends on productivity growth, and because most of our national income is in the form of wages, less capital translates into a lower national standard of living.

A double tax on any part of the economy is a bad idea. From the perspective of promoting long-term economic growth, a double tax on corporate profits is especially problematic. America's large corporations do the bulk of investment in capital equipment used in business and in research and development. Taxing profits takes away money that might otherwise be invested in income-producing and productivity-enhancing assets. And from the perspective of promoting trade competitiveness, taxing profits at the corporate level makes little sense since the corporate sector is the source of most of America's exports.

How much is our growth hampered by the corporate tax? This is extremely difficult to estimate, and as usual in economics the existing research suggests a wide range of possibilities. Despite the lack of hard numbers, there are two facts that should give us all concern.

First, even without the corporate tax, there is an inherent bias in our income tax system against saving and investment. Income taxation distorts our choice between consumption and saving. It makes consumption more attractive than it would be if a tax system were neutral. A consumption tax does not have this bias against saving and investment. And that is why economists concerned about improving economic growth will always prefer a consumption tax over an income tax. (Chapter 13 discusses consumption taxes.) Putting the corporate tax on top of the individual income tax adds yet another bias against saving and capital formation.

Second, the burden of the corporate tax on the domestic economy is a function of how responsive investment is to changes in the after-tax returns. If tax has little effect on investment decisions, there will be little impact on the capital stock that results from those decisions. One thing that is obvious is that capital has become increasingly mobile over the last few decades. Fifty years ago, the crucial decision for a corporation would be whether to build extra capacity in the United States or not at all. Now the main question is whether to build extra capacity in the United States or abroad. This increased mobility of capital means the damage the corporate tax can cause the economy is greater than before.

Problem 2: The Corporate Sector Suffers

Corporate investors don't want their hard-earned profits taxed twice. So they do all they can to avoid being classified as what is called a *Subchapter C corporation* (named for the part of the tax code dealing with taxable corporations).

To avoid the dreaded Subchapter C status, businesses potentially have three options. First, a business owned by one individual can operate as *sole proprietorship*. The owner simply includes business income on Schedule C of his or her individual income tax return.

Second, a business with more than one owner can operate as *partnership*. The partnership files a Form 1065, but no tax is levied at the entity level. The partnership sends each partner (and the IRS) a Schedule K-1. The K-1 informs the partner of his or her share of partnership income, deductions, and credits that needs to be reported on the partner's individual income tax return.

Third, a domestic corporation with less than 100 owners can be a *Subchapter S corporation*. The Subchapter S corporation files a Form 1120S with the IRS. Like a partnership it pays no tax and it sends each owner—in this case, each shareholder—a Schedule K-1. As with partnership profits, all Subchapter S profits flow through to owners and are taxed at each owner's individual income tax rate.

Each entity classification has its own advantages and disadvantages. For the most part, business owners want two things: (1) protection of their personal assets from bankruptcy and lawsuits and (2) protection of their profits from the corporation tax. Most small and medium-size business can achieve these goals by becoming an LLC, which is taxed as a partnership, or by adopting Subchapter S status. We will discuss these options in more detail in Chapter 10, but for now we will just lump all three categories of business not subject to corporate tax into one category called *pass-through businesses*.

The economic costs of the pass-through/corporate tax differences fall into two general categories. First, there are costs to businesses that are successful in avoiding Subchapter C status. These costs can take the form of the out-of-pocket expenses of hiring lawyers and accountants to be sure of not triggering any IRS rules that would have them reclassified as taxable corporations. Other costs of avoiding Subchapter C may not show up in a billing statement, but they are just as real. They are due to the lost efficiency of meeting the requirements of a filing or legal status that is not most advantageous from a pure (non-tax) business perspective. For example, to retain tax-free S corporation status, a business may have no more than 100 shareholders. For larger businesses, this limitation on ownership can severely restrict access to capital and raise costs.

Second, there are the costs to the economy that result when businesses cannot avoid corporate tax. Most large publicly traded companies are Subchapter C corporations for tax purposes. Their extra tax burden drives their after-tax rate of return below that of pass-through businesses. This provides incentive for investment to shift from the corporate sector to pass-through businesses. So, business lines that are commonly pass-through businesses—like your traditional "mom-and-pop" retailers—have significant tax advantages over businesses that must file as Subchapter C corporations. Contrast that with companies, say, in the aerospace industry, where both limited liability and access to the public capital market are a must. Government is thus interfering with the free market. If they could, our largest corporations would choose the pass-through model. The composition of investment is skewed away from its most productive mix.

Problem 3: Too Much Debt

Although a few corporations are debt free, most large and established corporations use a combination of debt and equity financing. When these corporations invest in capital, the returns generated are divided into returns on equity and returns on debt. By contract, debt must be paid on a pre-arranged schedule. Failure to make these payments on time means the corporation has defaulted and could end up in bankruptcy. Profit is a "residual"—the return on investment that is left over after obligations to debtholders have been met. The more debt the corporation has, the greater the risk of bankruptcy.

Only the return on equity is subject to corporation tax. Return on debt—that is, interest—is deductible and not subject to corporation tax. There is no economic basis for the tax differential. It is just one more arbitrary feature of the corporate tax. From an economic perspective, if we are going to have arbitrary taxation of corporations, we could just as well tax the returns to debt and equity, rather than just limiting the tax to returns on equity as we now do under current law.

The ratio of debt to equity is commonly referred to as the degree of a company's *leverage*. A simple and straightforward way for any corporation to minimize the tax on corporate capital is to increase leverage. By adding debt, the company increases its interest payments, which lowers profit and profit tax. This provides a strong incentive for corporations to borrow.

Relying too heavily on debt reduces a corporation's free cash flow. In an economic downturn or in times of extra volatility, a corporation might not have enough money to pay creditors. This can put a business in a financial straightjacket. Bankruptcy or even the threat of bankruptcy can result in major disruptions. If there is one lesson we have learned from the great financial crisis of 2007–2009, it is that too much debt can be devastating for a business. Because insolvency and illiquidity can spark a chain reaction, one major bankruptcy can threaten the whole economy. After the near-death experience for the economy, you might expect Congress to have a tax system that encourages less debt. Unfortunately, we have a tax system that does exactly the opposite.

The corporate tax's favoritism for debt also has another less dramatic negative effect on the economy. It favors industries that can support higher levels of debt over industries that cannot. Businesses with steady cash flows and lots of tangible capital that can be used as collateral—like public utilities—can finance a large proportion of their capital spending with debt. At the other end of the spectrum, risky investment in research and development must be financed almost exclusively with equity. And so, the corporate tax's bias in favor of debt gives tax advantages to staid debt-financed businesses over risky equity-financed businesses. Once again it seems we've got things backwards. In this modern world, where developing new technology is a policy priority, we should probably have a tax system that encourages equity over debt. But we have exactly the opposite.

Problem 4: Bias Against Dividends

Not all corporate profits are paid out as dividends. Some are retained earnings. In fact, some corporations, especially in the high-tech sector, pay no dividends at all. Shareholders who forgo dividends are hoping for larger capital gains.

The relationship between dividends and capital gains is inverse, and works like this: Suppose a corporation initially worth $100 earns $10 of profit. If the profits are paid out in dividends, the shareholders have $10 in cash and stock worth $100. If the corporation retains profits, on the other hand, the price of the stock should increase to $110 and the shareholders should hold $110 worth of stock.

In this sterilized example, the investor should be indifferent between capital gains and dividends. In reality, there is a world of difference between the two. When a company pays dividends, the shareholder decides where profits will be reinvested or whether they will frittered away on Caribbean vacations. When a company retains earnings, the corporation has control over funds. With huge sums at his or her disposal, a CEO can build an empire that could turn out to be a colossal success or failure. Whatever is decided—as long as executives can be trusted to have the best intentions for their shareholders—the government should not interfere. In the realm of tax policy, that means the tax treatment of dividends and capital gains should be equal.

Their tax treatment is not equal. Our fourth and final problem with the corporate tax arises not so much from the extra *burden* of the corporate tax but the extra *advantage* the corporate tax structure provides to capital gains. Corporate profits that filter through to individuals in the form of capital gains potentially have three tax advantages over profits paid out as dividends.

First, there is the possibility that the tax rate on capital gains is lower than the tax on dividends. Yes, under current law both dividends and capital gains are taxed at 15 percent. There is no rate differential. But we cannot ignore the possibility that this will change. If history is any indication, it is entirely possible that a differential could return in the future.

From 1913 through 1921, capital gains were taxed at the same rates as dividends and all other income. But from 1922 through 1986, capital gains were generally eligible for preferential treatment, usually in the form of a percentage of capital gains being excluded from taxable income. For example, from 1979 through 1986, the excluded amount was 60 percent of the gain. The Tax Reform Act of 1986 restored the equality of dividend and capital gains rates. But a differential soon returned. In 1990 and 1993, income tax rates rose generally while the tax rate on capital gains rates was capped at 28 percent. In 1997 the differential widened ever further. With the top individual rate on income (including dividends) at 39.6 percent, the capital gains rate was reduced to 20 percent.

In 2003, Congress for the third time in the history of the income tax equalized the tax rates on dividends and capital gains. But this time they were not set equal to the rates of tax on other income, but given a preferential rate of 15 percent. In current law, these rates are officially temporary. If Congress does not act, these rates will revert to pre-2003 levels at the end of 2012.

The second advantage capital gains on corporate shares have over dividends is a permanent fixture of the law. If current profits are not paid out as dividends, they are not immediately subject to individual tax. Individual income tax on corporate profit is deferred until the shareholder sells the stock and the gain is realized, or until the corporation finally decides to distribute it. Table 3-1 quantifies the benefit of deferral for a typical investment. In this example, if earnings are not distributed and the stock is sold 20 years later, the effective combined rate of tax on the original profits is 41.0 percent, compared to 44.8 percent if dividends were paid when profits were earned.

Deferring tax is always good, but exemption is better. The third advantage corporate capital gains can have over dividends occurs because any capital gains accrued are exempt from income tax at death. That is, the capital gain between the time the stock was purchased and the time of the purchaser's death is tax-free; heirs only pay income tax on gains from the time of death to the time they sell the stock. With no individual tax at all over the life of the original investor, the only income tax on profits for the original investor is corporate tax, and the effective rate is 35 percent. (Estate tax will also be due, but that's a whole separate controversy we won't get into now.)

Table 3-1. Tax Bias Against Dividends: Combined Individual and Corporate Tax Rates on Corporate Profits

Holding Period	Annual Dividends	Capital Gain (Sale)	Capital Gain (at Death)
10 years	54.8%	42.7%	35%
20 years	54.8%	41.0%	35%

Assumptions: Before-tax rate of return = 10%; corporate tax rate = 35%; dividend and capital gains tax rates = 15%

All of these biases against dividends create a "lock-in" effect. Individuals have a tax incentive to hold stock as long as possible. With higher taxes on dividends than capital gains, corporate executives have a tax excuse to retain profits. This could be considered a good thing if you want more savings. But inadequate corporate savings are not considered the problem. Experts in corporate governance believe managers are unduly predisposed to retain earnings. The corporate tax reinforces this tendency. This means that the corporate tax artificially limits opportunities for investment of funds those within managers' purview rather than the entire range of possibilities open to an investor.

Summary

The corporate tax wreaks all types of havoc on the economy. The economic case for repealing the corporate tax is rock solid. But, as we shall see in the next chapter, politics keep it a firmly entrenched fixture of federal finance.

CHAPTER

4

Why the Corporate Tax Won't Go Away

Obsolete, Unwanted, and Still Here

Okay, maybe the last chapter convinced you. It is crystal clear that the corporate tax is a disaster for our national competitiveness. What are we waiting for? Let's get rid of this rotten tax right away.

Well, besides the fact the government really needs the tax's $400 or so billion of revenue, and besides the fact that public is not as well educated as you in economics, there are a few details to deal with first. They may seem like mere technicalities, but these seemingly insignificant details could explode into big problems if not handled carefully. So, even if we want to, we can't just expunge the corporation tax from the Internal Revenue Code. What's worse and can be even more puzzling is the fact that eliminating the tax could make the tax law more complex than it already is.

Corporations as Tax Shelters

Here's the basic problem. The reason the corporate form exists is to provide a barrier between business and owners. Our legal system reinforces this separateness at every juncture. This separation of owner and business is great for capitalism but a headache for tax collectors. Without safeguards in the tax law that challenge this separateness, crafty individuals could use corporations to hide income and assets. In the simplest case, suppose an investor is earning $10,000 of interest from his portfolio of corporate bonds. Instead of holding the bonds directly, he can have a corporation that he owns hold the bonds. Now the corporation is earning interest income, and if the corporation (which he controls) does not pay dividends to the shareholders (he owns all the shares), there is no apparent income to the shareholder. Clearly this is a legal fiction with little economic substance. With his shell corporation he still must pay corporate tax, but as far as the individual tax is concerned, the investor has a created a tax-free savings account with no limits on its size or scope of investment.

To prevent wholesale abuse the IRS must ignore separateness. In situations where it perceives that corporations are being used as tax shelters, the IRS must pierce the corporate veil. It must establish the identity of the beneficial owner of the corporation. It must assign the income of the corporation to the shareholder, and tax that income as if the shareholder received the income directly.

There are already statutes to prevent the use of these "incorporated pocketbooks." These laws are left over from the 1930s when movie stars and other rich folks tried to use corporations to shelter income from rates that reached as high 78 percent. There is not much purpose for them now, as both the top individual and corporate rates are 35 percent. But if the corporate tax rate were eliminated—or even if the corporate rate dipped significantly below the top individual rate—all hell would break lose. There would be an avalanche of personal income pushing to get inside corporations, and an army of clever attorneys there to help. Little corporations could spring up in the millions for the sole purpose of avoiding income tax. So the corporate tax cannot simply be repealed without the IRS hiring more agents and Congress enacting complicated new rules to tax corporate income that is really personal income.

Integration of the Individual and Corporate Taxes

And it's not just intentional abuse we need to worry about. For the moment, let's assume that the natural human instinct to beat the tax man has been suppressed. The corporate tax has been repealed, and nobody is using corporations for the sole purpose of tax sheltering. The compliance problem may be gone, but there is still an economic problem.

At the other end of the spectrum from small, personal holding companies are large, publicly traded corporations—household names like Microsoft, Procter & Gamble, and Sunoco. These behemoths of American business did not incorporate to avoid taxes. All the same, if the corporation tax were abolished, the profits they don't pay out in dividends to shareholders would remain tax-free until those earnings were distributed or cashed out as a capital gain when shares are sold. If owners held shares until death, there would be no income tax on accrued gains at all. That wouldn't be fair to the rest of us paying tax. Moreover, it would reduce the productivity of the economy because there would be excess investment in businesses that have incorporated and inadequate investment in those that have not.

The seemingly straightforward way to address this problem is to tax corporate shareholders the way partners in a partnership are taxed. The partnership files a tax return, but this is mostly so the IRS can gather information. The partnership itself pays no tax. Partnership income is taxed once at the partner level. For large partnerships—like the nation's biggest law and accounting firms—this can create some intensely complicated tax calculations, as each of thousands of partners must be assigned his or her own share of income, credits, and other tax attributes that they must file include on an individual return. But the complexity is worth their trouble—and after all, they are lawyers and accountants—because it allows these large businesses to avoid corporate-level tax.

Under the *partnership model* of taxing corporate profits, all shareholders would report their apportioned share of the corporation's profit on their individual tax returns. The profits are taxed when earned, whether or not the shareholders actually receive cash dividends. The rate of tax on that profit is the individual tax rate that applies to their individual level of income. The partnership model would prevent use of corporations as tax shelters, and it would eliminate tax distortions that misallocate capital because no deferral of tax is allowed.

When the corporate and individual taxes are coordinated so corporate profits are taxed only once, it is called *integration* of the individual and corporate tax system. The partnership model is one type of integration. It eliminates the corporate tax. It is said to achieve *complete* integration because the shareholders of a corporation are taxed on *all* their corporate income as if the corporation did not exist.

Unfortunately, the partnership model is not practical for large, publicly traded corporations. A share of stock can have many owners in a single year—or even a single day. How do we assign corporate-level profits to each so they can report it on their individual tax return? And then there is the problem created by all the different types of corporate shares, and the problem of financial derivatives-based stock. How do we divide profit between different classes of stock? Tracking ownership and allocating profits at the end of each year would present near-impossible administrative and compliance burdens.

For this reason, most integration proposals only try to eliminate double tax when corporate income is distributed as a dividend (as opposed to when profit is earned). When relief from double taxation is provided only to dividends (not to retained earnings), it is called *partial* integration.

Although it is easier to implement than the partnership model, dividend relief is not piece of cake. And there is a lot of dispute among experts about the best way to do it. On one side are those who favor a *shareholder credit*. Under this method, when shareholders receive dividends, they also receive a tax credit equal to the taxes paid by the corporation. Corporations would compute tax no differently than they do currently. The corporate tax in effect becomes a withholding tax on dividends that are ultimately taxed at the shareholder level. The shareholder credit method is the approach favored by other countries that have adopted corporate integration. And it is the method endorsed by a prestigious group of academics and other experts in an influential 1993 report from the American Law Institute.

The main alternative to the shareholder credit method is *dividend exclusion*. Under this approach, corporations also compute tax no differently than they now do. But dividends are exempt from tax as long as it can be shown that the underlying profits were subject to corporate tax. This is the approach favored by the U.S. Treasury Department in its 1992 magnum opus on corporate integration.

There are other, more elaborate methods of corporate integration, such as the Treasury's Comprehensive Business Tax (CBIT), and the Business Enterprise Income Tax (BEIT) developed by Professor Edward Kleinbard of the University of Southern California. These will be discussed with other sweeping reform proposals in Chapter 14.

The (Non-)History of Integration

In the 1970s and 1980s, many foreign countries moved to integrate their corporate and individual income taxes. And for a while, all the momentum seemed to be moving in the direction that the United States would adopt a similar system. Experts in government and in the halls of academia put truckloads of intellectual effort into figuring out how to best integrate the corporate tax with the individual income tax. But it seemed every time their work was exposed to the political process, it was promptly dropped from serious consideration. Invariably, the problem was not so much strong opposition as a lack of support.

In July 1975, Treasury Secretary William Simon proposed a tax credit for shareholders equal to the estimated portion of corporate tax allocable to dividends. The plan was politely received and then filed away to gather dust. Later, in the waning days of the Ford administration, the Treasury Department released a plan for fundamental tax reform that included complete flow-through of corporate profits to individual shareholders. In a scenario that would repeat itself over the coming decades, it seemed that these proposals for corporate integration received praise mostly from academics and little from anybody else.

Democrats, too, supported the idea of integration. The Treasury Department under President Carter gave it considerable study, and in February 1978, House Ways and Means Committee Chairman Al Ullman (D-Oregon) introduced a plan for integration. It was a tax credit for shareholders equal to 10 percent of dividends. The percentage would be increased to 20 percent after six years. The details don't matter because the proposal was ignored.

In 1984, as the beginning of his effort to enact what would turn out to be the landmark Tax Reform Act of 1986, President Reagan proposed partial relief from double taxation in the form of a corporate deduction equal to 50 percent of dividends paid. As the bill wound its way through the legislative process it was scaled backed and finally dropped by the Senate.

Why were the proponents of integration repeatedly rebuffed? Paradoxically, the main impediment to their success was the group that would seem to have the most to gain—the corporate community itself. As noted in the prior chapter, in our tax system there has always been a significant bias against paying dividends. That was fine with executives. They like having a large cache of retained earnings that gives them a buffer against adversity and the flexibility to invest when and where they want. In particular, it gives them the power to buy other corporations. So whenever Congress gave them a choice between some newfangled relief for dividends and good-old tax incentives for new plant and equipment, they invariably chose the latter.

In 1992, the Treasury Department under President George H.W. Bush extensively studied the possibilities for corporate integration and made several proposals. Its final suggestion in the closing days of the Bush presidency was to leave the corporation tax untouched and—in a significant break from the trend in favor of a shareholder credit—recommended a dividend exclusion for shareholders.

The incoming Clinton administration, focused on deficit reduction and raising taxes on business and investors, had no interest in the Bush plan. But in 2002, President George W. Bush resurrected the dividend exclusion for inclusion in an economic stimulus package. His proposal provided an exemption for dividends to the extent that corporations actually paid tax. This required corporations to keep records that tracked previously paid corporate tax and assigned them to dividends. It would have been a significant new compliance burden for corporations and investors.

Ultimately, Congress dropped the Treasury plan and replaced it with a simple 15 percent individual tax rate on most dividends—irrespective of how much (if any) corporate tax was paid. This was significant tax relief for dividends, but the lack of coordination between corporate and individual payments made it an extremely crude form of integration. This proposal did provide some relief from double taxation, but it was poorly targeted and a far cry from the more sophisticated integration proposals that experts had worked out over the years.

The 15 percent rate on dividends (which was also provided for capital gains) was originally scheduled to expire at the end 2008. Congress passed legislation in 2005 that extended it to the end of 2010. Just before it was about to expire in 2010, Congress and President Obama agreed to extend the 15 percent dividend rate along with the other Bush tax cuts to the end of 2012. With budgets so tight and politics so heated, the fate of the 15 percent rate and other Bush tax cuts after 2012 is highly uncertain.

Meanwhile, countries around the world that had adopted shareholder credits have begun to reconsider. This is a result of tight budgets and increased competition for cross-border competition for investment. When it comes to packaging tax benefits for corporate profits, nations clearly prefer corporate rate cuts. Why provide tax benefits for shareholders who are unlikely to move because of high tax rates and whose portfolios have lots of foreign investment? Low corporate tax rates target incentives to highly mobile corporate capital.

Although it is nowhere on the political radar right now, we should keep in mind that the United States may also want to shift double-tax relief away from shareholders to corporations. Experts who were once strong supporters of shareholder relief are starting to reconsider. With multinational corporate investment moving easily from country to country, cutting the corporate rate creates more domestic jobs than dividend relief. Dividend tax relief is scheduled to expire in 2012, but any cut in benefits to dividends will be met with stiff resistance from influential investors and from Wall

Street. Still, with money being extremely tight, raising taxes on shareholders cannot be ruled out as a funding mechanism for corporate rate reduction.

The Case Against Any Corporate Tax Cut

The economic case against the corporate tax may be unassailable, but the political debate is far from settled. Several lines of reasoning—mostly from the political left—have been developed as arguments against any form of corporation tax relief.

First, there is what is known as the "entity view" of corporate taxation. All through the 19th century, the Supreme Court affirmed the principle that corporations were legal persons with many of the same rights as natural persons. If they enjoy the privileges of persons, why shouldn't they pay income taxes like other persons?

Proponents of corporate taxation often argue that the corporate tax can be justified by what economists call the "benefit principle." Corporations are legally separate from their owners. Corporations shield owners' personal wealth from liabilities that can arise from lawsuits and bankruptcy. When a partner dies or decides to leave a partnership, the business must be legally dissolved. A corporation has unlimited life, and its shares are freely transferable. The shares of the largest corporations trade on exchanges. Should corporations pay for the advantages they have over other business forms?

If the current corporate tax is justified by the benefit principle, it is not consistently applied. Many large corporations paying corporate tax are privately held and not traded on capital markets. Why should these businesses pay corporate tax? And on the flip side, there are large, publicly traded companies that are not subject to corporate tax. Why are these companies exempt? If the corporate tax is justified by the benefit of limited liability, why are millions of small corporations and LLPs that enjoy similar privileges exempt from corporate tax?

Another version of the benefit theory of corporate taxation looks to all the government services used by corporations and argues that it is only fair to charge businesses for these services. Again, there are holes in the argument. Why should these additional charges be targeted at large corporate businesses while millions of small businesses are excused? Why are only profitable businesses charged for services? And if the corporate tax is a fee, wouldn't you expect the bulk of the corporate tax to be collected from state and local governments, which provide the majority of government services? (States' receipts from their corporate taxes are only a fraction of the federal take.)

A third argument in favor of the corporate tax—and the one that probably carries the most weight—is that the corporate tax is necessary to keep the tax system fair. In this context, a fair tax system is one where the rich not only pay more tax than the poor, but they pay taxes at higher *rates* than the poor. A tax system with rates that rise with income is called "progressive," and "progressivity" is the guiding principle of tax policy for the political left.

Now, if you are going to use a fairness argument to support the corporate income tax, two things have to be true. First, you must believe a tax system should be progressive. That's a value judgment that depends on your own personal views.

Second, you have to believe that the burden of the corporation as a percentage of income is larger for high-income families than low-income families. In the past this was the view commonly taken by most economists. This follows from the assumption that investors will invest no matter what, and will simply have to absorb any tax increases that come their way. In recent years some economists have argued that a significant portion of the burden of the corporation tax falls on labor. This is consistent with the observation that capital is increasingly mobile over international borders. In other words, if there is a tax increase, a corporation can relatively easily move its operations across international borders, and those who will suffer most are workers who will lose jobs.

Who bears the burden of the corporate tax? Probably the best and most honest answer is that we really don't know. The uncertainty is so great that the Joint Committee on Taxation—the official scorekeeper for Congress on tax policy—simply does not include the corporation tax in its analysis of the distribution of tax burdens. Economists at the CBO also acknowledge the uncertainty. They address the problem by routinely presenting two distributional analyses of the burden of taxes—one where the entire burden is borne by the owners of capital, and a second where the burden is shared equally by labor and the owners of capital.

The Emotional Appeal of the Corporate Tax

So, it seems the noose is tightening around the neck of the corporate tax. Economists are now telling us that not only is the corporate tax terrible economics, but also that it may be hurting the working class. What more do you need to get the corporate tax repealed once and for all? The problem for would-be corporate tax cutters is that most Americans—even many conservatives—share the gut feeling that big business should pay income tax. There is no logic. But that's OK. We're talking politics.

If a magic ray gun from outer space turned us into a nation of rational robots, we would agree that corporations should pay no taxes. Any news report that a large corporation was paying no tax would be greeted with indifference. Our brains would tells us, "That's the way it is supposed to be," and we would change the channel. But no epidemic of rationality is likely to come soon. The idea that America's most profitable corporations don't pay their fair share of taxes is big news. It is one of the easier ways for journalists to stir up passions. It was true in the 1980s, and it is true now.

Let's take as an example General Electric—always near the top of the *Fortune* list of America's 500 largest companies. In 1984, General Electric made headlines when it was included on a list of prominent U.S. corporations that paid no income tax in at least one year between 1981 and 1983. The source of the information was a study by a labor-backed public interest group called Citizens for Tax Justice. To the tax profession it was hardly a shock that some corporations were not paying tax in the midst of a deep recession. But to most of the public it was an outrage.

Business groups vigorously disputed the methodology of the study. They complained, correctly, that the study did not report actual tax payments to the IRS (which are not public), but only "income tax expense"—an accounting concept that only roughly corresponds to actual cash payments. (I discussed this difference between actual and accounting tax expense in Chapter 2.) But who cares? Details may be important for analysis, but politics is more about impressions than facts.

The findings of the 1984 study of caught the eye of one prominent citizen. President Reagan had been a spokesman for General Electric in the 1950s. When his treasury secretary told him that General Electric and others big corporations were able to zero out their taxes, he replied, "I am surprised things have gone so far."[1] For the conservative president as well for the general public, General Electric's temporary tax holiday would be a clarion call for tax reform.

Fast forward to 2011. Global competition has made the case for corporate tax reduction stronger than ever. But the public outrage about big corporations escaping taxes has not abated. Again, General Electric is in the spotlight.

---

[1]Donald T. Regan, *For the Record: From Wall Street to Washington.* (New York, NY: Harcourt Brace Jovanovich, 1988), p. 153.

On March 24, 2011, the *New York Times* reported that General Electric's tax strategies "let it avoid taxes altogether." The story spread like wildfire over the Internet, over the airwaves, and through the halls of Congress. General Electric disputed many of the article's findings and pointed out that its low taxes were due to extraordinary losses in its financial business during the financial crisis. But, as in 1984, the damage was done. Most of the public, which knows and cares little about the intricacies of the corporate tax, now has the impression that many corporations pay little or no tax because they unfairly take advantage of tax "loopholes."

Summary

In short, despite the solid economic arguments against the corporate tax, public resistance to corporate tax relief is stiff. Corporations are not just separate entities and legal persons. They are *very powerful* separate entities. They are *very rich* legal persons. Invariably, a left-leaning politician points out that some struggling middle-class family pays more in income taxes than a huge corporation whose CEO makes tens of millions each year. No amount of economic reasoning can overcome the outrage fomented by that comparison. Public opinion is more easily swayed by one good story than a hundred economic studies. The world economy may be changing rapidly, but human nature stays the same. And as long as it does, we will have a corporation tax or something that looks a lot like it.

Cut the Rate!

The Easy, and Most Important, Part of Reform

Sometimes the corporate tax's tortuous tangle of rules and regulations can distract us from its most important feature: the tax rate. Unlike most everything else in corporate tax law, it is simple to understand. You can actually talk about it to regular people and they won't look at you like you're from Mars. And if lawmakers want to change it, all they have to do is adjust a few digits in the code, like resetting the temperature on your home thermostat.

It may be simple, but it is also a powerful policy tool. Currently the rate is 35 percent. If corporate capital is yielding 10 percent before tax, the after-tax return is 6.5 percent. By simply changing that "35" to a "25," the after-tax rate of return on *all* corporate investment increases to 7.5 percent. With heightened rewards for corporate investment, capital formation will increase, and along with it so will productivity and international competitiveness. The cost: Under current projections, the loss in revenue to Uncle Sam would amount to about $100 billion a year.

Now let's consider the difference between cutting the corporate tax rate and other types of corporate subsidies and tax cuts. Suppose that instead of reducing the rate from 35 to 25 percent we just gave the corporate sector $100 billion a year (with the amount allocated to each corporation in an arbitrary way—say, based on its market value). Corporations would be as happy to receive the $100 billion, and the Treasury as unhappy to lose it, as if there had been the rate cut. But there is one critical difference. With the rate still at 35 percent, there has been no increase in the after-tax return on investment. The government has spent $100 billion but has not increased the rewards for capital formation.

Let's take another example. Suppose that instead of rate reduction, the government provides $100 billion of "targeted" tax relief. Let's say that all industries using certain new technologies get the $100 billion of tax relief. The new tech sector is concentrated in the home districts of congressional leaders, and the public is fascinated with the amazing new technology. What's wrong with that, you say? Won't America prosper from giving the new technology a boost?

Well, in short, the answer to the last question is no. Sure, that subsidized tech sector will flourish and jobs will be created. Unfortunately, the visible job creation that proponents tout will be offset by invisible job losses spread through the rest of the economy, which does not receive a benefit. Unless you believe the government has better insight than the market about where future investment should be directed, the policy will change the composition of capital in unproductive ways.

Look at it this way. Put taxes aside for a second. The market takes all the investment opportunities out there and lines them up in order of profitability. Naturally, businesses choose the most profitable ones first and then continue down the line until the profitability of the last project does not exceed the cost of funding the investment. Now here's the beauty of the free market: what is best for private investors—the most profitable investments—is also what is best for the economy. The most profitable investments are the most productive. Following their own self-interests, businesses will choose the most productive mix of capital.

Now add taxes. Self-interested investors rank investments by the return they receive—their after-tax return. If the tax is uniform, taxation lowers the rate of return proportionately for all investments. In this case, businesses choose investments in the same order as before—that is, the most productive investments first.

If taxes are not uniform, low-tax investments rudely push their way to the front of the line and high-tax investments are forced back. When taxes are not uniform, less productive (low-tax) projects are undertaken while more productive (high-tax) projects are abandoned. Targeted tax relief leaves the economy with a less productive capital stock. Politicians and industry lobbyists always say the tax break they favor will promote productive investment. But that is just a sales pitch that defies economic logic.

These ideas are the guiding principles of tax reform. And they explain— much to the consternation of some business lobbyists—how tax reform can increase economic growth without cutting tax revenues. Sometimes cutting tax *rates* can be more important than cutting tax *revenue*. If targeted tax breaks are repealed and revenue gained is used to reduce tax rates, there will be no loss of revenue and the economy will grow more rapidly because its capital stock is more efficient.

Another benefit of rate reductions over targeted tax benefits is the difference in administrative and compliance costs. A targeted tax benefit requires rules to distinguish those who qualify from those who don't. These can take years to draft and can be fiendishly complex. And even still, audit disputes and court battles will often ensue. A tax rate cut requires no explanation.

Chicken Soup for the Code

Every tax system has its flaws and cracks. For political and technical reasons, it may can be extremely difficult to correct these problems. Lowering the tax rate is a simple way of reducing the effects of these problems without attacking them directly.

For example, suppose an island economy produces red grapes and green grapes. The island has a tax on business profits of 25 percent. Island leadership decides to provide a tax deduction for wages paid to workers in the green grape industry. With a tax rate of 25 percent, green grape growers get a tax subsidy of 25 cents for every dollar of wages paid. This creates a variety of economic distortions that overall reduce the island's productivity. Moreover, the red grape industry is unfairly penalized. But the green grape lobby is too strong to force repeal of the tax break. Instead of removing the subsidy directly, the subsidy could be reduced indirectly by cutting the tax rate.

Chapter 3 discussed many of the economic distortions caused by the corporate tax. Cutting the corporate tax rate would reduce their negative effects.

For example, by penalizing corporate investment, the corporate tax shifts the composition of investment to non-corporate business from the corporate sector. Small and midsize businesses distort their business practices and incur extra accounting costs to avoid being classified as a taxable corporation. Cutting the corporate tax rate would reduce the tax differential between corporate and non-corporate business and reduce inefficiency resulting from this differential.

Because interest costs can be deducted while dividend payments cannot, the corporate tax encourages corporations to finance investment with debt instead of equity. Reducing the corporate tax rate reduces the tax bias now in favor of debt.

Tax breaks complicate the code, make it less fair, and distort investment decisions. The value of tax breaks that come in the form of deductions—like accelerated depreciation and the special deduction for manufacturing (discussed in Chapter 7)—depends on the tax rate. Lowering the rate makes deductions less valuable, and their importance shrinks.

Tax shelters and tax planning thrive when tax rates are high. The tax benefits of this totally unproductive behavior are proportional to the tax rate. So cutting the corporate tax not only avoids the complexity that targeted tax breaks would entail, but it also reduces the complexity that results from all the complicated and costly maneuvers that corporations undertake to cut their tax bills.

One of these maneuvers is the adjustment of *transfer prices* for transactions between U.S. corporate parents and subsidiaries in low-tax countries (discussed in more detail in Chapter 9). Charging a low price for the transfer of goods or technology to a subsidiary in a tax haven shifts profits out of the United States and lowers the corporation's overall tax burden. The burden of complying with transfer-pricing rules is mind-boggling. But so are the benefits to corporations if transfer prices are carefully managed. A veritable cottage industry of transfer-pricing consultants has sprung up to service corporate America's needs. Cutting the corporate tax rate would reduce the benefit of transfer-pricing manipulation.

A Worldwide Trend

All the above are excellent arguments for cutting the corporate tax rate. They have been around as long as the tax has existed. But there is a new argument for cutting the rate that is as compelling, and it is easy for legislators to understand: over the last decade, corporate tax rates in foreign countries have dropped dramatically, and the trend is likely to continue.

Figure 5-1 tells the story. It shows the U.S. statutory corporate tax rate, including state taxes, from1981 through 2011. (Chapter 11 provides more about state corporate taxes, whose rates have averaged about 5 percent.) It also shows for the same period the average tax rate of four large Organisation for Economic Co-operation and Development (OECD) countries: France, Germany, Canada, and the United Kingdom; and the average for large cohorts of OECD countries (excluding the United States). Generally, countries with smaller economies have lower rates. Including them lowers the average.

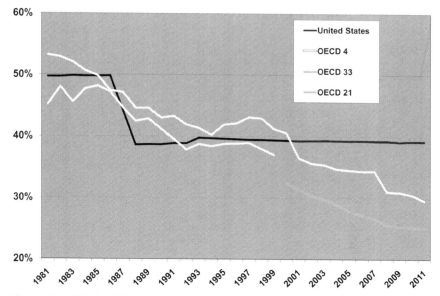

Figure 5-1. U.S. and OECD average corporate tax rates, 1981–2011. Source: Organisation for Economic Co-operation and Development.

After the Tax Reform Act of 1986 lowered the federal corporate tax rate from 46 to 34 percent, the United States had one of the lowest corporate tax rates in the world. But then things changed. Over the next quarter decade, foreign tax rates declined. Completely bucking the worldwide trend, the United States actually increased its tax rate from 34 to 35 percent in 1993. (If President Clinton had his way, the rate would have been changed to 36 percent, but Congress revised his original proposed rate downward.) And it has remained there ever since. The U.S. has a federal rate of 35 percent, and adding the average effect of state corporate tax rates raises the rate to 39.2 percent.

Table 5-1 shows that the United States has the second highest tax rate among all major economies. Only Japan's is higher. And if it weren't for the Great East Japan Earthquake in March 2011, the United States would have the top spot. The Japanese rate was scheduled to drop to 35.5 on April 1, but business leaders and the government have agreed to postpone the increase in light of Japan's need to fund reconstruction.

Table 5-1. Corporate Tax Rates (National and Local) in 2011

Country	Rate	Country	Rate
Japan	39.5%	Portugal	26.5%
United States	39.2%	Sweden	26.3%
France	34.4%	Finland	26.0%
Belgium	34.0%	United Kingdom	26.0%
Germany	30.2%	Austria	25.0%
Australia	30.0%	China	25.0%
Mexico	30.0%	Denmark	25.0%
Spain	30.0%	Netherlands	25.0%
New Zealand	28.0%	Switzerland	21.2%
Norway	28.0%	Greece	20.0%
Canada	27.6%	Poland	19.0%
Italy	27.5%	Ireland	12.5%

Source: Organisation for Economic Co-operation and Development

The four large OECD economies have an average rate of about 30 percent, and adding Japan to the average would raise it to 32 percent. Still, that leaves the United States with a corporate rate 7 percentage points higher than the other largest OECD economies.

The OECD average for 33 countries is about 25 percent—a whopping 14 percentage point difference from the United States. Advocates of rate reduction like to cite this figure, but it mildly overstates the problem because it gives small, low-rate countries—like Iceland and Slovenia—the same weight as large, higher-rate countries. Still, however you measure it, the once cutting-edge U.S. corporate tax rate is now out of date.

Luckily for the United States, tax rates aren't everything. Besides taxes, companies make location decisions based on the availability of skilled labor, wage rates, regulatory environment, infrastructure, and trade rules. And there is a lot more to taxes than just the corporate tax rate. But more than any other tax policy, a cut in the corporate rate sends a clear signal, especially to foreigners. It is an easy-to-understand indicator of a country's business climate.

For example, few experts outside of Ireland understand the intricacies of Irish tax law, but everybody involved in international business knows about its 12.5 percent corporate tax rate.

Why have the nations of the world gone on a rate-cutting binge? The answer you commonly hear is that they want to improve their competitiveness in an increasingly globalized world. This is certainly true, but there is more to it than that. Why are tax reductions in the form of *rate cuts* as opposed to other forms of corporate tax cuts, such as tax credits and more generous depreciation allowances?

One part of the answer relates to the transfer-pricing problem just mentioned. As world markets become more integrated, more corporations operate across borders. A larger portion of business is multinational. With the rise of multinational business, there are more opportunities for businesses to manipulate cross-border transfer prices and shift profits to low-rate countries. If a nation reduces its corporate tax, a multinational corporation has less incentive to move profits offshore. For example, if the U.S. reduces its tax rate from 35 to 25 percent, the tax benefit of transfer-pricing to Ireland (which has a 12.5 percent rate) is reduced from 22.5 to 12.5 cents on the dollar. This marginal incentive does not change with other tax breaks. If the United States provides accelerated depreciation or tax credits, for example, the benefit of shifting profits to Ireland at today's rates remains at 22.5 cents on the dollar. A nation can forestall erosion of its tax base by substituting lower rates for targeted incentives.

Rate Cuts vs. Incentives for New Investment

Despite all these arguments in favor of rate cuts, there are some economists who believe that rate cuts are not the best way to cut corporate taxes. They favor investment credits and other incentives that provide comparable benefits, such as accelerated depreciation. We'll talk more about investment credits and depreciation in the following chapter, but the important point to grasp now is that these incentives can be targeted to *new* investment—that is, they typically only provide tax benefits to investments made after an effective date. In contrast, rate cuts apply to the income generated after the effective date both from new investment and from investment already in place before the effective date.

Many economists consider it a waste of government money—a windfall— to provide tax relief for investment already in place. You cannot induce behavioral changes with tax benefits for "old capital"—as they call it. What's done is done. They prefer shutting out old capital and using the money saved to induce business decision-makers to invest prospectively.

This view is perfectly correct and compelling if your goal is maximizing capital formation. But there are other factors to consider. Incentives for new investment also have their shortcomings. For starters, they add considerable complexity to the code. Then, unlike a rate reduction, they do little to alleviate the debt-vs.-equity and corporate-vs.-non-corporate distortions. Furthermore, it can be difficult in practice to design them to be neutral across different types of investment, so they can create distortions across industries and across asset classes.

Finally, and perhaps most importantly, traditional incentives for new investment are best suited to provide incentive for businesses to expand existing investment projects to include relatively *low-profit, tangible* capital. In today's globalized business environment, governments want to attract *high-profit* investment projects that usually include a large amount of *intangible* investment. For example, if a multinational corporation wants to create blockbuster software, it will be more attracted to a locality with a low tax rate than with large incentives for plant and equipment. The next Microsoft wants low rates, not investment credits.

Critical Accounting Issues

Before concluding this chapter on corporate tax rates, it is important to highlight two accounting issues that you, as a savvy observer of the debate on corporate tax reform, will want to understand. Yes, this may not seem like the most thrilling topic but, as I have stressed, businesses and investors are nuts about reported accounting profits. How tax law changes are treated for accounting purposes is critical for determining whether corporations support or oppose particular proposals.

First, corporate tax relief in the form of rate reduction is far more advantageous to reported book profits than tax incentives that are due to timing differences. By far, the most important of these is accelerated depreciation of equipment. Accelerating depreciation does not increase the total amount of deductions, but does provide large financial benefit by providing them faster.

A cut in the statutory rate translates directly into a reduction in a corporation's effective tax rate and an increase in profits reported to shareholders. In contrast, accounting rules do not allow timing differences like accelerated depreciation to enter into the calculation of effective tax rates and book profits. So even though accelerated depreciation can result in a significant reduction in taxes paid to the IRS, it provides no increase in reported book profits. Accounting rules provide a strong incentive for corporations to prefer their tax breaks in the form of rate cuts rather than accelerated depreciation.

A second accounting issue that can greatly affect corporations' attitudes toward rate cuts involves what are known as the *deferred tax liabilities* and *deferred tax assets* that appear on their balance sheets. Deferred tax liabilities arise when for accounting purposes taxes are not paid on time (as when accelerated depreciation allows taxes to be deferred). In the world of accounting, they are past-due taxes.

Deferred tax assets arise when future taxes can be sheltered. They are like prepaid taxes. For example, in a year when a corporation has negative taxable income, that loss can be carried forward to shelter income in future years. That creates a deferred tax asset.

The size of many of these assets and liabilities is proportional to the corporate tax rate. For example, loss carry-forwards are less valuable if they are sheltering future income taxed at lower rates. If the corporation tax is reformed and rates are reduced, many deferred tax assets and liabilities shrink in value. The one-time change in value also gets recorded on income statements. So, for corporations with net deferred tax liabilities, a rate cut will reduce those liabilities, resulting in an increase in reported book profits. For corporations with deferred tax assets, a rate cut will reduce the value of those assets, resulting in a hit to reported book profits.

Because deferred tax assets and liabilities can be multi-billion-dollar entries on corporate balance sheets, these obscure accounting adjustments can have a large impact on a corporation's bottom line and on the degree of its support for corporate tax reform. For example, in 2004 a group of influential corporations successfully lobbied Congress to change a proposed rate cut into a revenue-equivalent deduction because they had large deferred tax assets. They did not want to report a large reduction in book profits that would result from the devaluation of those assets. Similarly, banks that had large losses during the last recession now have large deferred tax assets on their balance sheets. This means rate reduction could have a large one-time negative impact on bank profits.

Summary

The economic case for cutting the corporate rate is stronger than ever. And on Capitol Hill and in the business community, the chorus of support for a major rate cut could hardly be louder. But some companies with large deferred tax assets may not be so enamored of the idea. And enthusiasm will surely drop when those wonderful rate cuts are paired with not-so-wonderful cuts in tax breaks—the subject of the next two chapters.

Where the Money Is

The Big Corporate Tax Breaks

This chapter is about the three largest tax breaks for domestic profits: accelerated depreciation, the research credit, and the deduction for domestic production activities. Downsizing these three benefits will be the first thing legislators will look to pay for cuts in tax rates. But first, an important bit of corporate tax history.

The Investment Tax Credit

Before it was eliminated during our last corporate tax reform, the tax credit for the purchase of new equipment was the big kahuna of corporate tax breaks. In 1985, a year when total corporate tax collections were $61 billion, corporations generated $26 billion of investment tax credits. American business loved the credit. Businesses that bought capital equipment got an immediate tax credit equal to X percent of the purchase price of the equipment. In 1962, X equaled 7. In the 1980s the credit rate was 10 percent. Strangely enough, the "liberal" Kennedy administration was the driving force behind the credit's original adoption in 1962. And it was the "conservative" Reagan administration that was instrumental in its repeal as part of the Tax Reform Act of 1986.

Over its entire 24-year history, the credit stirred up passionate debate among economists. Some argued the credit did not stimulate investment. This group believed that the only factor important in investment decisions was capacity utilization. According to this view, capital spending would grow when business was brisk and sales growth strong. Other economists thought the credit had a large incentive effect on capital spending. According to this view, investment was very sensitive to the after-tax price of capital, and investment credit had a strong effect on price. As is often the case, the economic debate mirrored the political debate, with left-leaning economists arguing that the credit was just a windfall and right-leaning economists arguing it was a critical and influential policy tool. Most economists were willing to concede that price did matter at least to some degree, and the investment credit did indeed spur capital spending. But even now—after dozens of in-depth studies—there is no agreement about the magnitude of these effects.

One of the major objectives of modern economics is to control business cycles and the hardships they cause to millions. The British economist John Maynard Keynes (1883–1946) argued that the antidote to recession was strong government action. The government could stir up demand directly by spending more or indirectly by encouraging the private sector to spend more by cutting taxes. Tax cuts for individuals were used to stimulate consumer spending. Tax cuts for business were used to stimulate capital expenditure.

Time and again, the U.S. Congress used the investment credit as a tool for Keynesian policy. For example, in attempt to cool down an overheated economy, Congress temporarily suspended the credit from October 1966 to March 1967. And then it repealed the credit in April 1969, only to reinstate it in August 1971 to promote recovery from a recession.

In addition to its potential for helping the economy fight recessions by influencing demand, the investment credit was also a plus from the perspective of supply-side economics. Business investment increases the size of the capital stock. More capital increases productivity and wages. More capital improves competitiveness and long-term economic growth.

For all its demand- and supply-side potential, by the mid-1980s the investment credit had become frayed around the edges. Through the efforts of enterprising lawyers and accountants, the credit that was supposed to spur productivity was going to race horses and swimming pool equipment. Furthermore, economists complained that the credit was the cause of large distortions. Even though the credit for the most part was a flat 10 percent in the 1980s, it was hardly neutral in its treatment of different businesses. This occurred because investment in structures did not qualify for the credit and because a uniform rate tax credit is more beneficial for short-lived assets than long-lived assets. (That last fact is because a tax credit is a larger share of the cumulative lifetime income of a short-lived asset than of a long-lived asset.) So businesses that invested in short-lived investments were favored over those that made longer-term investment. Equalizing the tax benefits of different types of investments and different industries was a major theme of Reagan tax reform.

But probably the biggest factor leading to the demise of the investment credit was that it was the only tax break whose repeal generated enough revenue to pay for a major rate cut. In the end, the investment tax credit was a victim of its own success. With a credit rate of 10 percent and definition of qualified investment continually expanding, it was reducing corporate tax revenue by more than one-quarter. Once the Reagan administration committed itself to cutting the corporate tax rates, the revenue potential of the credit's repeal made commitment to repealing it unavoidable.

Accelerated Depreciation

The investment credit may be dead and buried, but its close cousin is alive and well. Accelerated depreciation provides a tax incentive for the purchase of new capital that is economically equivalent to an up-front tax credit. Let's look at how it works.

To measure profit correctly, businesses must deduct all expenses from gross receipts. One of their largest expenses is the declining value of the plant and equipment used use in production. For example, after a year of use, a piece of machinery purchased for $1 million may be worth only $900,000. The $100,000 decline in value is depreciation. This is an expense that reduces net income. Correctly measured, depreciation is referred to as *economic depreciation*. When tax depreciation is larger than economic depreciation, the corporation is getting a tax break.

Congress provides an incentive for the purchase of capital when it allows businesses to exchange larger depreciation deductions in the early years for smaller depreciation deductions in later years. True, total depreciation over the life of the asset does not change. It is just more accelerated. But the acceleration has considerable value. The delay in tax payments is the equivalent to an interest-free loan—money today in exchange for an equal amount of money tomorrow.

Table 6-1 provides an example. Let's assume a piece of equipment has a ten-year useful life and economic depreciation is $100,000 in each year. And suppose for tax purposes that this hypothetical machinery can be written off over five years using an accelerated pattern of depreciation. Measured in *constant dollars*, the tax benefits in early years are offset by tax losses in later years. But in *present value* terms—dollars that are discounted to take the time value of money into account—the net sum of tax benefits is the up-front equivalent of approximately $70,000. In other words, for the $1 million purchase of equipment in this example, accelerated depreciation is the equivalent of a 7 percent investment credit.

Table 6-1. An Example of the Value of Accelerated Depreciation

Year	Depreciation			Tax Benefit	Present Value of Tax Benefit
	Economic	Tax	Excess of Tax over Economic (All Numbers in Thousands)		
1	$100	$400	$300	$105.00	$105.00
2	$100	$300	$200	$70.00	$64.81
3	$100	$200	$100	$35.00	$30.01
4	$100	$50	−$50	−$17.50	−$13.89
5	$100	$50	−$50	−$17.50	−$12.86
6	$100		−$100	−$35.00	−$23.82
7	$100		−$100	−$35.00	−$22.06
8	$100		−$100	−$35.00	−$20.42
9	$100		−$100	−$35.00	−$18.91
10	$100		−$100	−$35.00	−$17.51
Total	$1,000	$1,000	$0.00	$0.00	$70.35

Assumptions: Assumes a tax rate of 35 percent and discount rate of 8 percent. The shaded cell is the tax benefit.

In practice it is difficult to know how much capital actually declines in value each year. Over the decades, the Treasury Department has devoted a great deal of time trying to measure economic depreciation in order to resolve its disputes with businesses. Gradually, concerns about accurate measurement—so difficult to accomplish—gave way to designing depreciation rules that were simpler and provided incentives for capital formation. Using its regulatory authority, the Treasury Department simplified and made depreciation allowances more generous in 1962 and again in 1971. Simplification usually occurs by reducing the number of categories of depreciable property. Depreciation allowances are made more generous by shortening depreciable lives and allowing more generous depreciation methods.

In 1980, Ronald Reagan made tax depreciation a major campaign issue. He proposed a "3-5-10" system, where all newly purchased capital would be depreciated over 3, 5, or 10 years. The Reagan administration eventually had to compromise by adding a 15-year category, but still the new depreciable terms provided write-offs much faster than economic depreciation.

The whole idea was to provide a powerful incentive for capital spending, and so it did. Combined with the investment tax credit, the post-1980 incentives were so large that the net corporate burden on profits from new capital purchases was negative. In other words, deductions and credits for the purchase of new capital equipment not only eliminated tax on profits on that equipment but could also be used to shelter other income. President Reagan's 1981 business tax was an astounding legislative victory. But in 1986 he would move 180 degrees in the opposite direction by decelerating depreciation allowances and repealing the investment credit.

Accelerated depreciation for equipment reduces Treasury receipts by approximately $30 billion annually. If it were repealed, the revenue pick-up could be used to reduce the corporate tax rate by approximately 3 percentage points.

Expensing

The fastest depreciation possible is the write-off of the entire purchase price of capital in the year of purchase. This is known as *expensing*. This treatment is so generous that many economists consider expensing capital investment equivalent to a tax exemption for the income generated by that capital.

Expensing plays two roles in the current tax system. First, it serves as a benefit for small businesses. It reduces their recordkeeping requirements, and it is an incentive for them to increase capital spending. In 2007, the limit on the amount of capital expenditure that can be expensed was increased from $25,000 to $125,000. As the result of several more recent changes in law, the limit increased to $250,000 for 2008 and 2009 and to $500,000 for 2010 and 2011.

The second role for expensing is to fight recessions (just as investment tax credit was used in the 1960s and 1970s). After the terrorist attacks of 2001, Congress allowed business the use of "partial expensing" (also known as "bonus depreciation"). As first enacted, businesses could immediately deduct 30 percent of the purchase price of an asset and depreciate the remaining 70 percent using normal depreciation methods. In May 2003 Congress temporarily increased the expensing percentage to 50 percent. As the economy recovered, partial expensing was allowed to expire on schedule at the end of 2004.

The financial crisis and consequent recession brought expensing back into service. In 2008, Congress enacted 50 percent partial expensing on a temporary basis. That was kept in place through September 2010. In December 2010—as part of the bipartisan legislation that extended the Bush tax cuts for two addition years—Congress took the "partial" out of partial expensing and allowed 100 percent of the cost of capital purchases made between September 2010 and the end of 2011. Currently, the expensing percentage is scheduled to drop back to 50 percent in 2012 and 2013 and then expire.

The Research Credit

Over and over, this book will stress the bedrock tenet of economics that no investment should receive advantageous treatment. Every lobbyist will tell you that the subject of his or her advocacy is an exception. Usually, this is a false claim. But there are cases where tax subsidies have genuine economic justification. This occurs when an investment provides spillover benefits to the public that are not captured by the business doing the investment.

Industrial research and development is just such a case. When a corporation conducts research, there is a social benefit—namely, new knowledge and technology—in addition to profit it yields to the business. Left to its own devices, the private sector will fund less research than is optimal for the overall productivity of the economy. So, unlike most other subsidies in the code, there is a solid economic case for the research credit.

The research credit first came into law in 1981. It has a unique *incremental* structure designed to provide maximum incentive effect per dollar of lost revenue. Let's use the incentive clause of a hypothetical basketball contract to illustrate the idea behind an incremental credit.

Say a team owner wants to provide an incentive for a rookie center to improve his free-throw shooting percentage. In college he shot a miserable 50 percent. He could give the player a flat $1,000 times the percentage of successful free throws in his season average (for example, $65,000 for a 65 percent average). But the owner can be pretty sure that he will not drop below 50 percent. So why give away $50,000 for free throws he would make anyway? Rewards for what will be done anyway do not change behavior. To economists they are just wasted money. To provide more incentive at lower cost, the owner could give the player $3,000 for every percentage point he gets over 50 percent up to 70 percent. Now the rookie gets $3,000 for each percentage point improvement. Using this incremental structure provides three times the marginal incentive at lower cost to the owner.

Unlike the investment tax credit, which equaled a flat percentage of the purchase price of equipment, the research credit is equal to a percentage of the excess of current expenditures over a *base amount*. Originally, the base amount was a three-year moving average of the prior three years' research expenditures. So, a corporation with $90, $100, and $110 of research over the prior three years would have a base amount of $100. If the current year's expenditures were $120, the creditable amount would be $20.

Over the years, Congress has made many modifications to the credit. Currently, businesses have three options for computing their research credit: (1) the "regular credit" with a 20 percent rate using a base period amount using qualified expenditures between 1984 and 1988; (2) the "alternative simplified credit" with a 14 percent rate and moving-average base; and (3) the "alternative incremental" credit, which is actually the sum of three credits with rates of 3, 4, and 5 percent and three different bases.

Adding to this daunting complexity is the uncertainty about the definition of qualified research. There can never be a bright-line test of what is qualified research and what is not. We probably can all agree that salaries of lab-coated chemists and the costs of their Bunsen burners are legitimate research expenses. But once you move out of a laboratory setting it gets difficult to make a distinction between research and other creative efforts. Software development is one particularly problematic area. The IRS is endlessly issuing new rules and fighting court battles that revolve around the definition of qualified research.

Of the three major tax benefits discussed in this chapter, the research credit is probably the least likely to ever be repealed. Every president since Reagan has endorsed the research credit, and there has always been strong bipartisan support for it in Congress. When it was originally enacted in

1981, Congress deliberately scheduled its expiration in five years so it could review the performance of its incremental structure.

Since then, a strange dynamic has developed. Invariably, when Congress needs to extend the credit, money is tight. To lower the estimated cost of legislation, Congress has gotten into the habit of extending the credit temporarily. Congress knows the credit has such widespread support that it will almost certainly be extended the next time it expires. And it is no secret that members of the tax-writing committee like to be lobbied by—and solicit contributions from—America's largest corporations who receive the lion's share of research credits.

Since 1981, the research credit has been scheduled to expire and extended 13 times. Only once during that period has the credit been unavailable—between midyear 1995 and midyear 1996. Most recently, Congress extended the credit when it extended the Bush tax cuts through 2012. But the credit was only extended through the end of 2011.

The credit costs the Treasury about $10 billion per year. In the unlikely event the credit is repealed (or allowed to expire), the revenue increase could be used to reduce the corporate tax rate by about 1 percentage point.

The Deduction for Domestic Production Activities

In the world of corporate tax breaks, the deduction for domestic production activities is the new kid on the block. Born when Congress passed the American Jobs Creation Act of 2004, the deduction was a by-product of a long-simmering international dispute.

Before the changes of 2004, the tax code provided an explicit subsidy for exports. The Extraterritorial Income regime (commonly known as "ETI") provided a partial exclusion for taxable income attributable to exporting. As the result of a complaint by the European Union, the World Trade Organization ruled that the ETI was a prohibited trade subsidy that violated the obligations of the United States to the WTO.

Congress repealed the ETI and replaced it with a deduction equal to a percentage of profits related to domestic production activity. Qualified activity included manufacturing, construction, engineering and architectural services, and software development. The number was 3 percent in 2005 and 2006 (effectively trimming the tax rate on qualified income from 35 to 33.95 percent). The deduction rate was increased to 6 percent in 2007 through 2009 (reducing the effective rate to 32.9 percent) and to 9 percent thereafter (reducing the effective rate to 31.85 percent). When gas prices spiked in 2008, Congress froze the percentage at 6 percent for oil-related production. As of this writing, President Obama and most Democrats in Congress want to repeal the deduction altogether for oil-related production.

It is not always easy to calculate the deduction for domestic production activities. There are complex rules for determining the activities that qualify as domestic production. Income from roasting and packaging coffee beans qualifies for the deduction, but income from sales of brewed coffee does not. Income from landscaping and house painting only qualifies if it is done in connection with construction, but otherwise it does not qualify. On top of definitional issues like these, domestic manufacturing income qualified for the deduction must be distinguished from foreign manufacturing income that is not qualified.

The domestic production activity deduction reduces Treasury receipts by about $15 billion annually. If it were repealed, the revenue pick-up could be used to reduce the statutory corporate tax rate by approximately 1.5 percentage points.

Summary

The three tax breaks highlighted in this chapter—accelerated depreciation, the research credit, and the deduction for domestic production activities—disproportionately benefit manufacturing and technology sectors. Corporations in these sectors purchase lots of equipment that qualifies for accelerated depreciation. They conduct the majority of the nation's research. And they have a lot of domestic production. A revenue-neutral corporate tax reform that cut these tax benefits to pay for lower rates would hurt these sectors.

At the other end of the spectrum, retailers, wholesalers, and financial corporations would generally see a significant tax reduction from a revenue-neutral reform. Because these companies' tax breaks are small compared with their profits, they generally would much prefer rate cuts to the status quo.

Although there are many variations of revenue-neutral corporate reform, any major effort would likely depend heavily on cuts to these three tax benefits. That will make it difficult for broad-based business coalitions like the Business Roundtable and the U.S. Chamber of Commerce to support revenue-neutral tax reform. That is why business has asked the administration to relax its requirement of revenue neutrality. And that is one reason why—irrespective of its policy merit—it is hard to be optimistic about corporate tax reform along the lines outlined by President Obama.

Corporate Tax Expenditures

The Hunt for Red-Hot Loopholes

"Tax expenditure" is the official name for a tax break. As the term implies, Congress can provide subsidies through the tax code just as well as it can through direct spending. For example, instead of the Department of Housing and Urban Development sending checks to developers of low-income housing, the IRS provides low-income-housing tax credits. Since the mid-1970s, government economists have put together a tax expenditure budget. These compilations are an extremely useful guide for tax reformers and anybody else who wants to see the size and scope of targeted tax relief.

Of course, one person's giveaway is another person's essential program. When government economists compile an official tax expenditure budget, they include all the deductions and credits that would not be part of an ideal income tax. But because there is no agreement about an ideal income tax, there is no agreement about what should be included on the list. Besides this problem of definition, there is also a problem of changing perceptions. When seen from a distance, the aggregated total of tax expenditures usually seems like a collection of special-interest loopholes. But upon closer inspection of each individual item, they often no longer seem so evil after all. Most of them are either widely available or advance goals popular with Congress and the public.

The sum of the annual cost of all tax expenditures is $1.1 trillion. The bulk of them are individual income tax benefits, including the exclusion for employer-provided health insurance, tax relief for retirement saving, the home mortgage interest deduction, and the deduction for charitable contributions. In the last chapter, we discussed the three most important corporate tax expenditures—accelerated depreciation for equipment, the research credit, and the special deduction for domestic manufacturing. The rest of this chapter discusses some other of the more important corporate tax expenditures. A complete list of the corporate tax expenditures and their revenue effects appears at the end of the chapter.

Some Not-So-Terrible Tax Breaks

It is easy to understand why popular tax breaks like the mortgage interest deduction and the deduction for charitable contributions would be nearly impossible to repeal. But what about those obscure corporate tax loopholes that are of no concern to most citizens? Surely once the light of day shines on them, lobbyists will be forced into the shadows and the spirit of reform will infuse the public.

Don't hold your breath. Base-broadening tax reform is truly a wonderful economic idea. But the bulk of corporate tax expenditures whose repeal tax reformers are counting on to pay for big cuts in the corporate rate are not all political poison. Far from it. The big three corporate tax expenditures in the last chapter have powerful political and economic justifications. Accelerated depreciation: Productivity growth. Research credit: High technology. Domestic production deduction: American manufacturing. Even if you are no friend of big business, these are hardly unsympathetic causes. The larger corporate tax expenditures not discussed in the previous chapter are described in the following sections. When subject to close scrutiny, most corporate tax expenditures simply do not conform to the image of special-interest tax giveaways that we hear from reformers.

Last-In, First-Out Inventories

To calculate profits, businesses must subtract the cost of the materials that went into the product. Purchased inputs are an investment in inventory that may not be deducted until they are actually used in production. An important issue for accountants is how to value the costs of inventory as it is put to use.

The two foremost methods of accounting for inventories are the first-in, first-out method (FIFO) and the last-in, first-out method (LIFO). Under FIFO, it is assumed when inventories are drawn down, the oldest items are used first. Under LIFO, it is the opposite—the newest items are assumed to leave first. Because prices generally are rising, FIFO's use of older items from inventory results in the lower expense of items drawn from inventory. Consequently, profits are higher. LIFO, using more recent prices, results in lower profits.

One of the classic debates in accounting theory is whether LIFO or FIFO is the better method of accounting for inventories. Neither is perfect. Ideally, businesses would deduct some average costs of items from their inventory when calculating their taxes. One argument strongly in favor of LIFO is that it corrects for the overstatement of income due to inflation. If prices rise 10 percent annually, a business using FIFO that deducts one-year-old (lower-priced) inventory has artificially inflated profits. Its revenues are inflated, but its costs are not.

LIFO largely eliminates this problem. It eliminates the income measurement problems caused by inflation. Ideally, the corporate tax would exclude *all* inflationary gains. Opponents of LIFO argue that providing an inflation correction exclusively for inventories is not justified unless the entire code made corrections for inflation.

With no clear-cut policy case for repeal, the debate about LIFO is probably best framed in terms of money. The CBO estimates that repeal of the LIFO method (and another profit-cutting inventory accounting method known as "lower of cost or market") would raise approximately $98 billion over ten years. (Most of this pick-up is in early years because the proposal requires recapture over four years of LIFO reserves. These reserves represent the excess profits accumulated over the years, because the oldest and least-cost items in inventory were assumed to have never been used in production.) Some of the main beneficiaries from the availability of LIFO are the major oil companies. There is little doubt LIFO will be among the most discussed revenue-raisers in any serious corporate tax reform effort.

Graduated Corporate Tax Rates

To keep things simple, up until now I've been saying the corporate rate is 35 percent. That's not a bad approximation, because more than 90 percent of corporate profits are taxed at that rate. But as with the individual income tax, the corporate rate structure is graduated—high levels of taxable income pay higher levels of profit—as shown in Table 7-1.

Table 7-1. The Graduated Corporate Rate Structure

Tax Bracket	Taxable Profits Between . . .
15%	$0 and $50,000
25%	$50,000 and $75,000
34%	$75,000 and $100,000
39%	$100,000 and $335,000
34%	$335,000 and $10 million
35%	$10 million and $15 million
38%	$15 million and $18.3 million
35%	$18.3 million and above

Source: Internal Revenue Service

You may have noticed the 39 percent "bubble" for profits between $100,000 and $335,000 and the 38 percent "bubble" for profits between $15 and $18.3 million. They're put there to erase the benefits of the initial lower rates for large corporations. In effect, corporations with more than $18.3 million in profits pay a flat rate of 35 percent.

These special low tax rates for low-profit businesses are not included in the tax expenditure budget because they do not qualify under the definitional rules. But they are a simple and clear giveaway to one privileged class of businesses. In the individual income tax, graduated rates are an essential feature of a tax system that tries to extract "equal sacrifice" from low- and high-income families. But low rates for one class of corporations have no similar justification. They may do little or nothing to promote progressivity, as many rich people own small corporations and many lower-income families own stock in *Fortune* 500 companies.

Eliminating the graduated corporate rate structure is often mentioned as a possible revenue raiser in corporate tax reform. It was included in the Wyden-Coates proposed tax reform (discussed in Chapter 1), and it regularly appears in the CBO's annual list of possible revenue raisers. Requiring all corporate profits to be subject to the 35 percent rate would raise about $2.5 billion annually.

Low-Income Housing, Tax-Exempt Bonds, and Charitable Contributions

The low-income-housing tax credit reduces corporation taxes by about $5 billion a year. Tax-exempt interest on state and local bonds reduces corporate tax by about $9 billion a year. And deductions for charitable contributions reduce corporate taxes by about $3 billion a year. These three tax benefits are grouped together here because they share a common feature. Although they significantly reduce corporate taxes, corporations are not the primary beneficiaries.

In the case of low-income-housing credits and tax-exempt bonds, corporations get tax benefits, but at the same time they give up some pre-tax profits to get these tax benefits. Corporations' net benefit—that is, the tax benefit minus reduced receipts—is small. The benefits from the government-provided tax relief flow through to third parties in the form of reduced rents for the residents of low-income housing and lower rates of interest for the state and local governments issuing bonds.

Similarly, if the deduction for corporate charitable contributions were cut, it would only hurt the organizations on the receiving end. Any attempt to scale back these popular tax breaks would meet stiff resistance from sympathetic parties that the public does not associate with big business.

Oil Company Tax Breaks

With gas prices exceeding $4 a gallon in the spring of 2011, President Obama and Democrats in Congress pushed hard to repeal many tax benefits for oil and gas producers. In addition to a proposal to repeal LIFO, President Obama's most recent budget proposed repealing nine other tax benefits for oil companies. The largest of these are described below.

Percentage Depletion

Depletion is to oil well owners what depreciation is to manufacturers. It is a deduction for the decline in value of their investment property. Real depletion is even harder to measure than economic depreciation because you can never be certain how much oil is under the ground, and therefore how much to value the extraction of oil. There are two main methods of accounting for depletion. Under *cost depletion,* a fraction of a well owner's cost of investment is deducted each year, where the fraction is a rough estimate of the percentage of the well's reserves extracted in that year. Under the often much more generous *percentage depletion* method, depletion is arbitrarily assumed to be equal to a fraction of gross income from the well. This often gives the owner deductions over the life of the well far in excess of the original investment.

In the 1956 movie classic *Giant*, as Rock Hudson and his oil-rich buddies share cocktails around the swimming pool, they toast the 27.5 percent oil depletion allowance. Those heady days of humongous tax breaks for big oil are long gone. The percentage was reduced to 22 percent by the Tax Reform Act of 1969. In 1974, with gas prices and oil profits soaring, percentage depletion was repealed entirely for big oil companies (called the "integrated majors"). Under current law, percentage depletion is only available to independent producers, and the allowable deduction varies from 5 to 22 percent of gross income from a producing property. Percentage depletion costs the Treasury about $1 billion annually.

Expensing of Intangible Drilling Cost

In addition to the cost of the oil-producing property itself, oil companies incur significant costs for preparing and drilling wells. These costs—mostly in the form of wages, fuel, supplies, and repairs—are investments that should be capitalized and deducted over the life of the well. But current law allows these expenses to written off immediately, except for bigger oil companies, which must spread 30 percent of the costs over 5 years. Disallowing expensing of intangible drilling costs is estimated to raise $8.5 billion over 10 years.

Deduction for Domestic Production

This deduction, discussed in the previous chapter, is not limited to oil companies. However, while it is generally equal to 9 percent of profits for other businesses, the deduction is only 6 percent of profits for oil companies. The repeal of the domestic manufacturing production for oil companies is estimated to raise $15.9 billion over 10 years.

Limitation on Tax Credits for Foreign Taxes Paid by Oil Companies

As discussed in the following chapter, U.S. companies are taxed on their worldwide income. But to prevent double taxation of foreign profits, the

United States grants a tax credit roughly equal to foreign taxes. There are always disputes about what constitutes a creditable foreign tax. Income and profits taxes generally qualify. Excise taxes generally don't. But in the wide world of taxation there are a lot of in-betweens.

The creditability of taxes on oil company foreign profits is particularly problematic. In countries where a company is extracting oil, it will pay royalties for the rights to pump the oil (usually on a per-barrel basis), and it may also pay profit taxes. This two-pronged relationship with the host country government makes the oil company a "dual-capacity taxpayer." Royalties—considered a normal cost of business—are not creditable. Without restrictions, foreign governments and oil companies would negotiate contracts where companies only paid foreign governments (creditable) profits taxes instead of (deductible) royalties. The dividing line between royalties and creditable foreign taxes is a hotly contested issue. The Obama administration proposes to limit creditable foreign taxes to taxes paid by all businesses in that country; special taxes on oil production would no longer be creditable. The proposal is estimated raise $9.2 billion over ten years.

On May 17, 2011, the Senate took up the issue of repealing these tax breaks for the five integrated majors—ExxonMobil, ConocoPhillips, Chevron, Shell, and BP. To prevent the legislation from being killed, supporters needed 60 votes, but they only got 52 votes—most of them from Democrats. But it isn't over yet. This issues is unlikely to disappear from public view, as Democrats love to juxtapose tax breaks for high-profit big oil companies with Republicans' proposed cuts in social programs.

Incentives for Alternative Energy

Tax subsidies for alternative energy serve two policy goals: (1) to reduce air pollution and greenhouse gas emissions, and (2) to promote energy security by reducing dependence on oil from foreign sources. In general, they enjoy widespread support.

Republicans like tax subsidies for alternative energy because they are tax cuts. Democrats like them because they can help reduce global warming. Everybody wants to reduce dependence on foreign oil.

Unfortunately, tax subsidies are fundamentally flawed tools for achieving these goals. There are two reasons why. First of all, none of these tax subsidies encourages us to conserve energy in the most basic ways—turning off lights, driving less, taking stairs instead of the elevator. Second, in promoting only specified alternative technologies, they put Congress in the position of picking winners and losers in one of the fastest-growing and most unpredictable sectors of the economy. Suppose an entrepreneur develops software that promotes more efficient distribution of electricity. Because the innovation is not associated with any of the technologies identified by Congress for a subsidy, it gets no government support.

When it comes to reducing something, a tax on that something is more efficient than a subsidy to substitute for that something. A carbon tax is a far better method of reducing global warming than subsidies for alternative energy. It promotes conservation as well as new technology, and it doesn't pick any favorites among existing and future technologies. Similarly, to promote independence from the potentially debilitating economic effects of swings in oil prices, a tax on petroleum products is a more efficient solution than a subsidy for oil substitutes. To quiet the uproar from the rise in energy prices that would result from any tax, revenues from the new taxes could be distributed to the public as refundable tax credits.

Even with a 100 percent rebate of the revenue to the public, carbon and other broad-based energy taxes currently have little political support. In contrast, tax subsidies for all types of alternative energy have grown rapidly over the last decade, despite the growing drumbeat for tax reform and for getting rid of tax breaks for special interests. Now there are more than a dozen subsidies for alternative energy in the tax code—some for individuals, some for business, and some for both. The following paragraphs describe three of the more important of these for corporations.

Credit for Investment in Clean Coal Facilities

The term "clean coal" has several different meanings. It may refer simply to the more efficient burning of coal through pulverization and gasification. It may refer to "scrubbing" coal free of chemical pollutants like carbon dioxide. Or it may refer to advanced processes that allow carbon dioxide to be removed from coal emission and sequestered. The clean coal credit is available for all these technologies. It came into law as part of the Clean Energy Act of 2005. It can only be utilized by corporations with projects approved by the Department of Energy. A total of $1.65 billion of credits is available under that legislation.

Production Credit for Wind Energy

Wind turbines on top of towers hundreds of feet tall are becoming increasingly common on the American landscape. You can thank U.S. tax law. Most investment in wind power would not be economically viable without the alternative energy production tax credit. The credit is equal to 2.2 cents per kilowatt hour of electricity generated for the first ten years of the life of a production facility. Currently, the production tax credit is set to expire at the end of 2012.

Investment Credit for Solar Energy

The sun's energy can be harnessed for electric production directly with photovoltaic cells or by concentrating the sun's energy to generate steam to move turbines. Solar energy can also be used to heat buildings, homes, and pools. The main tax subsidy for solar energy is a tax credit equal to 30 percent of the purchase price of solar equipment. The credit is currently scheduled to expire at the end of 2016.

Production and investment credits are also available for other less widely employed alternative energy sources, including investments in geothermal power generation, qualified hydropower facilities plants, microturbine power plants, and combined heat and power property. Also, facilities fueled by biomass, landfill gas, and trash may be eligible for tax credits.

Until recently, banks and other financial companies have been among the largest investors in wind and solar products. The tax credits helped reduce their tax liabilities as their profits soared in the heady days before 2008. When the bottom dropped out of the financial services industry, it also caused a crisis in the wind and solar energy sectors. Financial firms without tax liability could no longer use the credit. As a result, investment in alternative energy projects dried up. In response, Congress allowed investors, for 2009 and 2010 only, the option of receiving a cash grant from the Treasury in lieu of tax credits for wind, solar, and other alternative energy sources.

The status of alternative energy tax breaks seems to be in a constant state of flux. Most the benefits are temporary. Every year or two there is another energy tax bill that creates new subsidies, modifies existing ones, and temporarily extends those that are expiring. This is a source of great frustration to the industry. But it keeps the lobbyists in Washington fully occupied.

Conclusion

A strong case can be made that some provisions of the tax law that are considered tax expenditures—such as LIFO and the deduction for charitable contributions—are not expenditures at all but legitimate business expenses.

For the most part, however, there is a good economic case for repealing most tax expenditures. Naturally, lobbyists will put up a fight to retain them. But it is also likely the public will lose much of whatever zeal it had for reform when it learns that many of these tax expenditures are not sinister tax loopholes, but subsidies for causes that enjoy widespread support.

Chapter Appendix:
The Corporate Tax Expenditure Budget

Table 7-2 gives a complete list of the 84 corporate tax expenditures, as compiled by the Office of Tax Analysis of the U.S. Treasury Department and reported in the president's Budget for Fiscal Year 2012. Dollar amounts are in millions.

Table 7-2. The Corporate Tax Expenditure Budget

Tax Expenditure	2010	2011	2012–2016
Deferral of income from controlled foreign corporations	$38,130	$41,410	$212,840
Accelerated depreciation of machinery and equipment	17,140	5,400	109,440
Deduction for U.S. production activities	10,010	10,510	62,450
Exclusion of interest on public-purpose state and local bonds	9,850	8,990	73,120
Credit for increasing research activities	5,770	3,850	10,320
Credit for low-income-housing investments	5,370	5,690	34,270
Expensing of research and experimentation expenditures	3,220	4,250	32,960
Graduated corporation income tax rate	3,000	3,280	17,840
Inventory property sales source rules exception	2,680	2,910	18,770
Deferred taxes for financial firms on certain income earned overseas	2,330	0	0
Exclusion of interest on life insurance savings	1,500	1,570	9,220
Deductibility of charitable contributions, other	1,370	1,430	8,430

Tax Expenditure	2010	2011	2012–2016
than education and health			
Energy production credit	1,370	1,430	7,810
Exemption of credit union income	1,270	1,240	7,920
Exclusion of interest on hospital construction bonds	1,140	1,040	8,490
Special ESOP rules	950	1,030	5,950
Work opportunity tax credit	860	770	1,050
Excess of percentage over cost depletion, fuels	830	910	4,930
Exclusion of interest on bonds for private non-profit educational facilities	760	690	5,620
Temporary 50 percent expensing for equipment used in the refining of liquid fuels	760	620	–1,700
Special Blue Cross/Blue Shield deduction	750	715	3,120
Excess of percentage over cost depletion, non-fuel minerals	720	740	3,560
New markets tax credit	650	720	3,160
Deductibility of charitable contributions (education)	620	650	3,950
Tax credit for orphan drug research	470	550	4,630
Exclusion of interest on owner-occupied mortgage subsidy bond	400	360	2,950
Expensing of exploration and development costs, fuels	350	460	2,010
Exclusion of interest on rental housing bonds	340	310	2,510
Tax incentives for preservation of historic structures	300	300	1,600
Exclusion of interest for airport, dock, and similar bonds	270	250	2,020
Credit for investment in clean coal facilities	240	400	1,770
Tax exemption of certain insurance companies	200	200	1,070

Tax Expenditure	2010	2011	2012–2016
owned by tax-exempt organizations			
Credit for holders of zone academy bonds	190	200	790
Exclusion of interest on student-loan bonds	180	160	1,310
Deductibility of charitable contributions (health)	180	190	1,130
Expensing of certain small investments	170	960	−1,310
Advanced energy property credit	160	540	1,060
Alternative fuel production credit	160	160	270
Exclusion of interest on bonds for water, sewage, and hazardous waste facilities	150	130	1,100
Expensing of multiperiod timber-growing costs	150	180	970
Empowerment zones and renewal communities	150	100	600
Credit for energy-efficient appliances	150	60	0
Natural gas distribution pipelines treated as 15-year property	120	120	430
Amortization of all geological and geophysical expenditures over two years	120	90	190
Exclusion of interest on small-issue bonds	110	100	780
Expensing of exploration and development costs, non-fuel minerals	110	110	660
Exemption of certain mutuals' and cooperatives' income	110	110	600
Energy investment credit	100	120	3,560
Tax credit and deduction for clean fuel–burning vehicles	70	40	170
Exclusion of interest on bonds for highway projects and rail-truck transfer facilities	60	60	270
Alcohol fuel credits	60	70	260
Deferral of gain on disposition of transmission	−50	−150	−520

Tax Expenditure	2010	2011	2012–2016
property to implement FERC policy			
Allowance of deduction for certain energy-efficient commercial building property	50	60	230
Exclusion of gain or loss on sale or exchange of certain brownfield sites	50	40	60
Employee retention credit for employers in certain federal disaster areas	50	20	10
Special alternative tax on small property and casualty insurance companies	40	40	200
Special rules for certain film and TV production	40	20	30
Tax credit for certain expenditures for maintaining railroad tracks	40	20	30
Qualified school construction bonds	30	60	740
Small life insurance company deduction	30	30	150
Accelerated depreciation on rental housing	–30	–30	–110
Industrial CO_2 capture and sequestration tax credit	20	30	450
Credit for holding clean renewable-energy bonds	20	20	100
Deferral of gain on sale of farm refiners	20	20	100
Deferral of tax on shipping companies	20	20	100
Credit to holders of Gulf Tax Credit bonds	20	20	60
Biodiesel and small agri-biodiesel producer tax credits	20	10	0
Expensing of environmental remediation costs	10	–110	–540
Deduction for endangered species recovery expenditures	10	20	140
Exclusion of interest on energy facility bonds	10	10	50
Exclusion of utility conservation subsidies	10	10	50
Expensing of certain multiperiod production costs	10	10	50

Tax Expenditure	2010	2011	2012–2016
Expensing of reforestation expenditures	10	10	50
Investment credit for rehabilitation of structures	10	10	50
Credit for disabled-access expenditures	10	10	50
Exclusion of interest on veterans housing bonds	10	0	50
Credit for construction of new energy-efficient homes	10	10	10
Welfare-to-work tax credit	10	10	0
Employer-provided child care credit	10	0	0
Qualified energy conservation bonds	0	0	50
Expensing of certain capital outlays	0	10	50
Tribal Economic Development bonds	0	10	40
Recovery Zone bonds	0	0	0
Accelerated depreciation of buildings other than rental housing	−2,440	−2,950	−16,190

Source: President's Budget for Fiscal Year 2012

CHAPTER 8

How Should Foreign Profits Be Taxed?

Growing Controversy, Growing Importance

What do Microsoft, General Electric, Cisco, Merck, and Google have in common? All of these icons of American business now earn more than half of their profits outside the United States. As shown in Table 8-1, ten years earlier most of their profits had been domestic. More than ever before major U.S. corporations are truly multinational businesses. These companies may lobby for the research tax credit and other domestic tax breaks, but it is the tax treatment of foreign profits that is by far their most important tax issue. Far more than any other factor, low taxes on their foreign earnings contribute to the low effective tax rates they report to shareholders.

Table 8-1. Foreign (non-U.S.) Share of Worldwide Profits of Some Leading U.S. Multinationals

	1998–2000 Average	2008–2010 Average
Microsoft	17%	60%
General Electric	39%	82%
Cisco	33%	79%
Merck	28%	57%
Google*	--	58%

* Google did not become a public company until August 2004.

Foreign Profits: To Tax or Not to Tax?

Economists always want a level playing field, but in international taxation the playing field is hopelessly bumpy. Countries set their own tax rates. They deliberately try to tilt the playing field in their favor to attract investment. The disparity in tax rates raises the question of how to tax profits when a corporation is headquartered in one country and does business in another. Should the tax rate of the home country or host country prevail?

Naturally, each nation taxes business taking place within its own borders. The United States taxes Toyota on its operations in the United States. And Germany taxes IBM on its operations in Germany. The most vexing question of international taxation is, How should a nation tax its multinationals on their foreign profits? Should Japan tax Toyota on its U.S. operations? Should the United States tax IBM on its German profits?

There is no simple answer. Consider the relevant example of a U.S. corporation with a 35 percent domestic tax rate and a 20 percent foreign rate. If the United States adds a 15 percent tax to foreign profits, both domestic and foreign profits are taxed at equal rates. This is referred to as the "worldwide" approach to international taxation. The good thing about this approach is that it creates a level playing field between domestic and foreign investment undertaken by U.S. corporations. There is no tax incentive to locate operations abroad. But then there is this: if U.S. corporations pay a 35 percent tax while foreign competitors pay 20 percent, there is a significant competitive disadvantage for U.S. companies operating in foreign markets.

The major alternative to the worldwide system is known as "territoriality." Under this approach, the United States would only tax corporate profits generated inside its borders. Foreign profits of its U.S. multinationals would not be taxed by the United States. Foreign profits would only be subject to the 20 percent tax imposed by the host government. This puts U.S. companies on equal footing with foreign competitors. Both pay 20 percent. But now the U.S. company is not tax neutral in its choice between domestic and foreign investment. It has a tax incentive to locate operations outside the United States.

For as long as there has been a corporate tax, there has been a fierce debate about whether territorial or worldwide taxation should be the guiding principle of international tax policy. In practice, the U.S. system has been a compromise between the two. In the 1960s, the Kennedy administration proposed that the United States move to a pure worldwide system. It did not succeed. But as a compromise, Congress did agree to raise taxes on foreign profits in situations where inappropriate tax avoidance was likely. A quarter of a century later, the Tax Reform Act of 1986 tightened foreign tax rules even further.

More recently, the pendulum has definitively swung in the opposite direction. Many of the rules instituted in 1962 and in 1986 have been undone by a combination of legislation, regulation, and crafty tax planning. At the same time, in order to promote the competitiveness of their multinationals, most other countries have gone even further and adopted territorial systems. Currently, there is tremendous pressure on Congress from the business community to the do the same for U.S. multinationals.

Key Features of U.S. Taxation of Foreign Profits

The two most important features of U.S. international tax law are the *foreign tax credit* and what those in the trade refer to as *deferral*—the ability to avoid paying U.S. tax on foreign profits until those profits are paid back as dividends to the U.S. parent company.

Structurally, the U.S. tax system is that of a worldwide system. The U.S. claims the right to tax all the income of its residents and resident corporations no matter where it is earned. In a worldwide system, the foreign tax credit prevents double taxation. It works like this. If a corporation earns $100 of foreign profit in a country with a 20 percent rate, it pays $20 of foreign tax. The home country also taxes that profit at, let's say, a 35 percent rate. But to prevent double taxation, the home country grants the corporation a foreign tax credit of $20 for the $20 of foreign tax paid. The net after-credit home country tax of $100 of foreign profits is $15. Total (foreign and domestic) tax is $35. The multinational pays the same amount of tax whether profits are earned at home or abroad. This can make life tough for home country multinationals trying to compete in a worldwide marketplace.

Although U.S. corporations technically are subject to worldwide taxation, effectively they have most of the benefits of a territorial system. This is primarily because of deferral. The United States does not tax foreign profits as they are earned. Foreign subsidiaries incorporated under foreign laws effectively shelter foreign profits from U.S. tax. In general, the United States does not "see" any foreign profit unless and until the U.S.-controlled foreign subsidiary pays a dividend to its U.S. parent. U.S. taxes on foreign profits are deferred until repatriated to the United States. Deferral can generate significant tax advantages. In fact, the ability to defer paying U.S. tax on foreign profits until profits are repatriated allows foreign profits of U.S. multinationals to almost entirely escape U.S. taxation.

If foreign tax rates were roughly equal to the U.S. rate, deferral would not provide much of a benefit. But in general that is not the case. Except for corporations engaged in mining, oil drilling, and natural gas extraction, taxes on foreign profits of U.S. multinationals have been falling and are now generally low. This has occurred for two reasons. First, foreign countries have reduced their corporate tax rates. Second, multinationals have been extremely successful in shifting their profits from relatively high-tax countries like France and Germany into low-tax countries like Luxembourg and Ireland. The combination of minimal U.S. tax and low foreign tax makes foreign investment very attractive to U.S. multinational corporations.

Deferral can have a large impact on a corporation's reported effective tax rate and on its book profits. Although potentially liable to U.S. tax, unrepatriated foreign profits are considered exempt from U.S. tax for accounting purposes. If a multinational designates foreign earnings as being "permanently reinvested"—even though in reality they are only indefinitely kept abroad—no U.S. tax liability needs to be subtracted from reported profits. Reported effective tax rates of U.S. multinationals have declined dramatically in recent years. By far the largest factor behind this development is the increasingly advantageous tax treatment of foreign profits.

But there is a price. To keep foreign profits free from U.S. tax, multinationals must not repatriate those profits back to the United States. This incentive to keep earnings offshore is called the "lock-out effect," and it has a significant impact on the way a multinational manages its funds. In practice, unless there are sufficient foreign tax credits to offset the U.S. tax liability that awaits them at the border, U.S. multinationals are extremely reluctant to repatriate foreign profits. As a result, U.S. corporations have accumulated over $1 trillion of foreign earnings in foreign jurisdictions.

Should Foreign Profits Get a Holiday?

If a multinational's foreign profits are locked out, it cannot use foreign earnings to pay dividends to its shareholders. It cannot use foreign earnings to acquire U.S. companies. And it puts limits on cash that be used for domestic investment and job creation.

In response to these concerns, Congress in 2004 gave U.S. multinationals a "one-time" tax holiday for foreign profits repatriated to the United States. For one year, foreign subsidiaries could pay dividends to U.S. parents and pay only 5.25 percent U.S. tax. American corporations brought back $362 billion under provisions of this law. Most of the repatriated money was used to pay dividends, repurchase shares, and acquire other corporations. There is little evidence that the provision fostered domestic capital formation or created any new jobs. An attempt to enact a second holiday for foreign earnings was defeated in the U.S. Senate in early 2009. But a coalition of America's largest multinationals continues to seek a repatriation holiday and argues that it will foster much-needed U.S. job creation. But there is little reason to think a second round of tax relief will be any more successful than the first.

Should the United States Adopt a Territorial System?

Business has been lobbying for decades for the United States to adopt a territorial system, and those efforts have moved into high gear since Japan and the United Kingdom adopted territorial systems in 2009. But like so many things in tax law, the devil is in the details. Multinationals' support for such a change depends on exactly how the rules are written.

In 2005, the president's Advisory Panel on Tax Reform and the congressional Joint Committee on Taxation both floated proposals that would put the United States on a territorial system. But both these proposals were estimated to *raise* revenue! This current U.S. system is so generous to corporations that entirely exempting foreign profits from U.S. tax would be a tax hike! Obviously, American corporations do not want a territorial system that raises their taxes. What they want is a territorial system like the one adopted in the United Kingdom. This would cut their taxes.

Why do the 2005 territorial proposals raise revenue while a system like the United Kingdom's loses revenue? The main difference is how exempt foreign profit is measured—in particular, whether or not expenses related to foreign income can be deducted from U.S. income. Under widely accepted accounting principles, expenses should always be matched with income. The *matching principle* is a fundamental principle of U.S. tax law. One corollary of the matching principle is that no deduction should be allowed for expenses that are used to generate tax-exempt income. (With income from investment A already exempt, such a deduction would reduce taxes on investment B.) So, for example, interest on loans that are used to purchase tax-exempt securities is not deductible.

Many expenses incurred in the United States can be related to foreign profits. A portion of expenditures on research and of salaries incurred at U.S. headquarters are expenses that contribute to foreign profits. And, because money is fungible, interest on domestic debt frees up capital that helps finance foreign operations. The two 2005 territorial proposals adhere to the matching principle. Accordingly, because foreign profits would be exempt, the deductions for the portion of expenses allocable to foreign profits would be disallowed. Under the generous U.K. territorial system, deductions for expenses related to foreign income *are* allowed. A system that allows deductions for expenses allocable to exempt income is so generous that it no longer taxes foreign investment, but subsidizes it.

Now all of this sounds pretty arcane, but it is absolutely essential for understanding the debate about the future of U.S. international tax policy. A territorial system with deduction disallowance rules is a tax increase vehemently opposed by business. Without deduction disallowance rules, a territorial system is a tax cut business would warmly welcome.

Should the United States Raise Taxes on Multinationals?

It is a sign of our unsettled times that while there is much talk of entirely exempting foreign profits, there are also serious proposals to *increase* tax on foreign profits. The tax expenditure budget includes three major items concerning foreign-source income that could be repealed to pay for a reduction of the corporate rate or for deficit reduction.

Deferral of U.S. Tax on Unrepatriated Foreign Profits

Originally proposed by the Kennedy administration, repeal of deferral would subject all foreign profits of U.S. multinationals to U.S. tax. The United States would have a true worldwide system. The impact of such a change is largest for corporations with low foreign taxes.

Large businesses abhor the idea. It is totally unacceptable to them. They consider it a relic from the past. They argue that it is out of touch with reality, given that most other countries have moved in the opposite direction and adopted territorial regimes. But repeal of deferral still has a few proponents. For any chance of political viability, it must be coupled with rate reduction. The Wyden-Coats tax reform plan, which reduces the corporate rate to 24 percent, includes repeal of deferral. And some economists have estimated that repeal of deferral by itself could on its own reduce the corporate tax rate to 28 percent in a revenue-neutral reform.[1]

Deferral of Foreign Finance Profits

No matter how much a country may want to give tax relief to foreign profits, it must protect its domestic tax base. It must always be on guard against corporations shifting truly domestic profits to foreign jurisdictions. Accordingly, one of the most basic anti-abuse rules in international tax law is to prevent passive income from portfolio investments from getting the same favorable treatment given to active foreign profits. If foreign passive income went untaxed, there would be a mass migration of investment accounts to offshore locations. Even your most fervent advocates of tax relief for multinationals acknowledge this.

In practice, it is not always clear where the dividing line is between passive and active investment. The problem of distinguishing the two is most acute in the financial services sector. For example, when a bank manages a portfolio of business loans, are the profits active or passive? In 1986, Congress basically said all foreign financial service profits were passive and therefore could not get the benefit of deferral. In 1997, Congress reversed itself and allowed a large amount of financial service income to be considered active

---

[1] Harry Grubert and Rosanne Altshuler, "Corporate Taxes in the World Economy: Reforming the Taxation of Cross-Border Income," paper prepared for the James A. Baker III Institute for Public Policy Conference, "Is It Time for Fundamental Tax Reform?: The Known, the Unknown, and the Unknowable," December 2006.

and therefore eligible for deferral. This allowed large American banks to substantially reduce their worldwide tax rates.

President Clinton tried to rescind the 1997 change by exercising his line-item veto—a power newly granted by Congress in that year. But the Supreme Court subsequently ruled the line-item veto unconstitutional. Now, what is known in the trade as the "active financing exception" is a prominent fixture in the Washington lobbyist scene. Like the research credit, it is popular with business and repeatedly extended on a temporary basis. It is currently scheduled to expire at the end of 2011 and is estimated to cost the Treasury nearly $5 billion annually.

Foreign Sourcing of 50 Percent of Profits from Exports

As noted in Chapter 7, Congress in 2004 repealed the ETI export incentive in response to pressure from the European Union. But the EU did not catch everything. U.S. tax law still retains one other incentive for exports. The incentive works by allowing some exporters to get extra foreign tax credits. It works like this. Under U.S. law, foreign tax credits cannot exceed 35 percent of foreign profits. Corporations that are constrained by this limit dearly want to enlarge foreign profits. Under any reasonable rules about sourcing the profits from exports, most export profits would be attributed to the United States where most of the value was created. But U.S. rules generously deem half of those profits foreign. This favorable export profit source rule has no expiration. The Treasury estimates that this rule reduces federal revenue by $7.5 billion a year.

Repeal of these tax expenditures is too blunt an approach even for most Democrats who want to raise taxes on multinationals. Instead, they have proposed targeted reductions in foreign tax credits and deferral. By far the most noteworthy are those from President Obama. These proposals would, according to a May 4, 2009 Treasury Department release, "ensure that our tax code does not stack the deck against job creation here on our shores."

Obama Administration Proposals

During the 2008 presidential campaign, President Obama made the tax treatment of foreign profits a high-profile campaign issue. In his 2009 and subsequent budgets, his administration has outlined a number of highly technical proposals that would raise nearly $200 billion over ten years by reducing foreign tax credits and the benefits of deferral. One proposal would eliminate deferral for extraordinarily high profits from intellectual property parked in tax-haven holding companies. Another would limit profit shifting from high-tax to low-tax foreign countries. And yet another would limit U.S. tax deductions until associated profits are subject to U.S. tax. American multinationals have lobbied vigorously against these proposals, so Congress has shown little willingness to follow through. Only one of President Obama's proposals to increase corporate taxes on foreign profits has become law, and this change is expected to raise only $10 billion over 10 years.

CHAPTER 9

Globalization and the Modern Multinational

The World Is Getting Smaller

Falling trade barriers and rapid reductions in the costs of communication have transformed the way large American corporations do business. National borders don't matter so much anymore. Fifty years ago, most research and manufacturing was done in the United States. And the bulk of revenues came from sales to U.S. customers. Foreign sales subsidiaries were organized along national lines. Today, vast amounts of U.S. multinationals' production capacity, and even some research, have shifted overseas. Between 1980 and 2010, the number of manufacturing jobs in the United States dropped from 19.2 million to 11.6 million. Modern multinational operations are highly interdependent. Various components of a product line many be manufactured in different countries, and there may only be one supply chain for that product worldwide. Sales forces are organized regionally. In this environment, there is more intrafirm international trade.

In addition to an increase in the scope and scale of cross-border operations, another major difference of modern corporations from those of yesteryear is the increased prominence of intellectual property (IP). These "intangibles" can be legally sanctioned like patents, trademarks, and tradenames. Or they can appear in less formal (though not less valuable) guises, such as know-how, customer lists, and workforces in place. The corporate giants of the past like U.S. Steel and General Motors generated value through economies of scale in production. Many modern corporations like Microsoft, Apple, and Merck generate their value from IP created through research and development (as in the case of patents) and massive marketing efforts (as in case of tradenames).

Both globalization and the bigger role played by intangible property vis-à-vis plant and equipment have had huge implications for the taxation of large corporations. The opportunities to move both real operations and paper profits to low-tax jurisdictions have multiplied, and U.S. corporations are taking advantage of them.

Jobs and International Tax Rules

There are two overarching facts that you will never hear from lobbyists for U.S. multinationals. First, it is true that the combination of low foreign tax rates and the ability to defer taxes on foreign profits does create a significant tax incentive for U.S. corporations to move production and jobs to low-tax countries. With the U.S. corporate tax at 35 percent and the Irish rate 12.5 percent, and with the ability to indefinitely defer U.S. tax, there are obvious tax advantages for a U.S. corporation to locate production in Ireland over the United States.

Second, it is true that America's multinational corporations are moving jobs out of the United States. As shown in Figure 9-1, U.S. multinational corporations cut their domestic employment by 1.9 million. Over the same period U.S. multinationals increased their employment overseas by 2.4 million between 1999 and 2008.

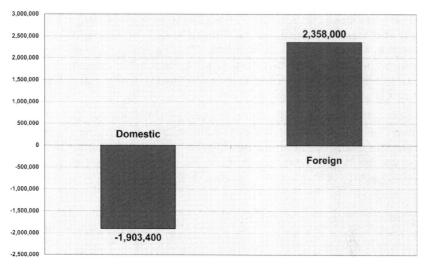

Figure 9-1. U.S. multinational job creation, 1999–2008. Source: U.S. Department of Commerce.

During the 2008 presidential campaign, Barack Obama took these two facts and used them to imply U.S. tax rules were the cause of the hollowing out of American manufacturing. And after his inauguration, the president followed through on campaign promises to do something about it. In early 2009, he made several proposals to curtail tax benefits for U.S. multinationals. In a May 4, 2009, press release, the White House stated: "Our tax code actually provides a competitive advantage to companies that invest and create jobs overseas compared to those that invest and create those same jobs in the U.S."

But there are other issues to consider. Before the rush to limit foreign tax credit and deferral, we should try to understand the quantitative effect taxes have had on the job exodus and the potential for President Obama's proposals to create jobs. Furthermore, we must take into consideration the possibility that foreign investment could have some beneficial impact on the U.S. economy.

Many factors besides taxes—including wage rates, infrastructure, energy costs, and proximity to markets—enter into a corporation's decision of where to locate a production or distribution facility. There are good reasons to believe that these other factors have played a larger role than tax differences in the loss of U.S. manufacturing jobs from the United States.

First of all, just as a matter of arithmetic, wages are almost always a much larger expense for business than income taxes. And the opportunities for wage reductions are much larger than they are for tax reductions. For example, wage bills can be cut by as much 90 percent by moving production from the United States to China or India. Tax benefits from rate differentials are small potatoes in comparison.

Second, only a fraction of the countries where multinationals are increasing employment are low-tax countries. In China and India, tax rates are not especially low. In these countries, the influence of wage rates clearly dominates any tax benefits. In other countries where growth in foreign employment has been large—such as in Western Europe—the main draw is access to large consumer markets.

Though taxes may not be the largest factor in explaining employment shifts, they cannot be ignored either. They do play a role in plant location decisions, as any drive through the Irish countryside or the villages of Switzerland will make crystal clear. Low-tax Ireland is a favored location for manufacturing operations of U.S. high-tech and pharmaceutical companies. Low-tax Switzerland is increasingly used as the location for European headquarters of U.S. corporations.

But total employment by U.S. corporations in Ireland is only 85,000. In Switzerland, it is only 45,000. Obviously this job creation is not responsible for the millions of jobs losses in the American Midwest. Moreover, not all of these jobs can be considered lost U.S. jobs. Many of these jobs would be in Ireland and Switzerland even without low tax rates. Furthermore, many of these jobs—if not in low-tax Ireland of Switzerland—would be outside the United States anyway. So, while favorable international tax rules could be a small contributing factor to U.S. job loss, they cannot be blamed for the decline in American manufacturing.

Finally, to the extent that low taxation of foreign profits has increased foreign investment by U.S. companies, some of that foreign investment can have positive effects for U.S. job creation. Business groups and some economists argue that jobs created by foreign investment are more numerous than the jobs lost. According to their view, the United States can create more jobs at U.S. headquarters and research facilities if multinationals have a strong foreign presence. The larger the potential market for U.S. goods that incorporate U.S. technology, the more U.S. companies will invest in research. In effect, tax-favored foreign subsidiaries serve as "export platforms" for U.S. goods, services, and technology.

U.S. multinationals argue that foreign investment does not substitute for domestic investment. On the contrary, greater investment abroad means greater domestic investment and job creation in America. So tax breaks for foreign investment increase foreign jobs *and* domestic jobs. If they do not have tax advantages comparable to multinationals based in foreign jurisdictions, multinationals argue that they will not be able to compete in foreign markets and will have to cut domestic employment that supports foreign sales.

In summary, U.S. tax law does gives American companies an incentive to locate operations abroad. But it is unlikely that this alone has had any significant impact on the overall employment picture. Much more significant than the outmigration of jobs is the outmigration of the domestic corporate tax base, discussed in the next section.

The Price Is Not Right: Profit Shifting

Affiliates within a multinational enterprise are in a state of continuous interaction. They provide each other goods, services, and a wide variety of IP. For tax purposes, it necessary to tally profits separately in each country in which the multinational operates. So when an affiliate in Country A ships goods, provide services, or allows use of its patents to an affiliate in Country B, affiliate A must charge affiliate B just as if they were unrelated parties. If the charge is fair, there is a fair allocation of profits. If A charges too much, profit is shifted from B to A. If A charges too little, it is the other way around. These intracompany, interaffiliate charges are generally referred to as *transfer prices*.

In practice there is usually a wide range of possible transfer prices, and a great deal of controversy between corporations and tax officials about which price within that range should be used. The stakes are large. Transfer pricing is not a detail. By adjusting transfer prices, multinational corporations are able to shift huge amount of profits from high- to low-tax countries and substantially reduce their worldwide tax bills.

The following sections illustrate some examples of how this is done.

Example #1: Irish Manufacturing

Suppose a U.S.-headquartered corporation has an affiliate that manufactures computer components in Ireland. It costs the Irish subsidiary $10 to produce the component. The United States incurs $60 of marketing and other costs for the sale of each product. The ultimate sale price to outside customers is $100. The question is how the $30 of profit will be allocated between Ireland and the United States.

The IRS determines by looking at comparable operations and sales between unrelated parties that a reasonable return for the Irish subsidiary would be 50 percent over costs, or $5 per component. Therefore, a reasonable price for sales from the Irish subsidiary to the U.S. parent is $15 per item.

The U.S. multinational and its transfer-pricing consultants, however, assert that the scientists in Ireland have made significant improvements to the product, and, with no help from the U.S. parent, Irish engineers have streamlined the manufacturing process. The company also argues that because of advances made by competitors, the U.S. patent rights shared with Ireland years ago no longer have much value. It also asserts that the U.S. tradename is unknown to the public outside the United States.

For all those reasons, the multinational asserts the correct transfer price is not $15 but $25. After a heated battle, the IRS finally agrees to the claim because it is under pressure to settle cases promptly and because it does not have the resources to properly review all transfer-pricing disputes. That leaves the Ireland subsidiary with profits ($15) at triple the appropriate level ($5). The inflated profits are subject to low Irish tax rates, rather than higher U.S. rates. This lowers the company's effective tax and increases after-tax profit.

Example #2: Patent Transfer to Bermuda

A U.S. pharmaceutical company anticipates that concerns about excessive levels of a certain protein in human blood will soon be a major health issue in the United States. It also realizes that, as the result of prior research, it has already developed a compound (intended to treat an unrelated ailment and never brought to market) with the "side effect" of reducing that protein.

The remaining additional product development, including drug trials, will take place in the United States. The compound will be sold primarily in the United States, where the company already has a well-trusted name and an extensive U.S. sales force. Without any tax planning, all profit from the new product would be generated in the United States.

The U.S. corporation decides to set up a company in Bermuda to hold the patent rights to the new drug. To achieve that, the Bermuda affiliate must "buy into" the rights to the existing compound by making an up-front payment. Because the previously disregarded compound had been considered to be nearly worthless (with respect to its intended use), valuation experts are able to make the case that the buy-in payment from the Bermuda affiliate—and therefore the U.S. profit from the sale of the technology—should be small. Subsequent research payments by the Bermuda subsidiary are not large relative to expected sales revenues.

The hoped-for result is soon realized. The repackaged compound is a blockbuster, and most of the profit is attributed to the Bermuda subsidiary where the patent legally resides. The company is able to do that because it successfully argues that most of the profit was created by the Bermuda-funded research.

Example #3: Luxembourg Lending

Besides adjusting transfer prices, multinationals can also shift profits across borders by lending from one affiliate to another. Consider a U.S. company that has a profitable subsidiary in France. It also has an affiliate in low-tax Luxembourg. The Luxembourg affiliate makes a loan to its French sister that is large enough to ensure that interest paid by the French firm to the Luxembourg company nearly eliminates profit in France. The business profit formerly generated in France has been transformed into interest earnings for the Luxembourg subsidiary. Consequently, profits avoid French tax and become subject to very low tax in Luxembourg.

In the not-too-recent past, this type of "foreign-to-foreign" profit shifting was harshly penalized under U.S. ta rules. Prior the late 1990s, if the two related affiliates on each side of the loan were corporations, the United States taxed the interest immediately. Instead of paying tax to the high-tax country, as it was doing before the loans, the corporation would have to pay tax to the United States. Now it is easy to get around this rule. Under "check-the-box" regulations promulgated by the Clinton Treasury, the U.S. parent can deem the Luxembourg subsidiary an unincorporated branch and avoid U.S. tax. This allows the shifting of profits to a tax haven without any U.S. taxation.

These examples are highly simplified representations of real international tax planning. It was recently reported that Google used a complicated structure known as a "double Irish Dutch sandwich."[1] Between the U.S. parent company that developed the key software and the foreign subsidiaries making regional sales of advertising, Google placed an operating subsidiary considered Irish (under U.S. law) and Bermudian (under Irish law), a Dutch holding company, and an Irish holding company. The transfer of IP into this structure allowed Google to reduce U.S. tax on income from the U.S.-developed intangible property, reduce Irish corporate tax, avoid Irish withholding tax, and

---

[1] Jesse Drucker, "Google 2.4% Rate Shows How $60 Billion Lost to Tax Loopholes," Bloomberg, October 21, 2010.

avoid U.S. tax rules that penalize related-company royalty payments. Google's reported worldwide tax rate over the last three years was about 23 percent, and its foreign tax rate averaged about 3 percent.

The Magnitude of the Profit-Shifting Problem

Surveys of tax managers of multinational enterprises consistently show that transfer pricing is their single most important international tax issue. And there is little doubt that that transfer pricing is one of the leading, if the not the number one, issue for the IRS in its dealings with large businesses.

The data confirms the widespread success of cross-border profit shifting. Profits gravitate to jurisdictions with low tax rates. Table 9-1 presents the data on the profitability of affiliates of U.S. multinational corporations in five low-tax countries. In all these jurisdictions, the average effective tax rate on U.S. affiliates was below 10 percent. These are all small jurisdictions, their economies equal to about 1 percent of the world's economy. But, as small as they may be, together they account for 24 percent of foreign profits of U.S. multinationals. Their rates of profit are many multiples of those of other countries with higher tax rates.

Table 9-1. High Rates of Profit in Low-Tax Jurisdictions

	Before-Tax Profits	Average Tax Rate	Profits per Employee
Bermuda	$16.2	2.6%	$5,404,333
Singapore	$14.6	7.4%	$115,422
Ireland	$45.4	7.7%	$488,730
Switzerland	$18.2	9.1%	$219,217
Cayman Islands	$7.4	9.4%	$1,123,333
Five-tax-haven total	$101.8	7.2%	$326,230
World total	$430.2	29.6%	$42,947

Source: Bureau of Economic Analysis, U.S. Department of Commerce.

There is also evidence that the Treasury's revenue losses from transfer pricing is growing. Figure 9-2 shows that the degree of income shifting out of the United States has risen. From 1999 through 2007, foreign profits of U.S. multinationals have increased by 163 percent, while over the same period traditional indicators of economic activity have increased by far less: sales grew by 101 percent; tangible property, plant, and equipment grew by 50 percent; and employee compensation grew by 66 percent. This trend is particularly pronounced for multinational corporations whose profitability depends heavily on intangible assets. Annual reports filed by many pharmaceutical and high-tech companies show declining worldwide tax rates, with a significant swing in the share of profits booked abroad, without a commensurate increase in real foreign business activity. All the data strongly suggest U.S. multinationals are readily able to shift profits into tax havens and thereby significantly reduce taxes properly owed to the United States. Estimates of the annual revenue loss from transfer pricing vary from $30 billion to $60 billion.

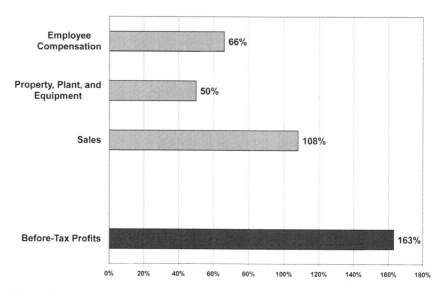

Figure 9-2. Growth of Foreign Affiliates of U.S. Multinationals, 1999–2007. Source: Bureau of Economic Analysis, U.S. Department of Commerce.

Summary

What can the government do to reduce excessive profit shifting? There are no easy solutions. There is little doubt that increasing IRS resources to improve staffing would help. But if anything, it appears Congress will be cutting rather than increasing IRS budgets. Some have advocated that the federal government adopt a "formulary" approach, similar to that used by U.S. states and Canadian provinces, to apportion income on the basis of measurable quantities, like sales, assets, and payroll. (State formulary apportionment is discussed more in Chapter 11.) Because multinationals have few real business activities in island havens like Bermuda and the Cayman Islands, this could eliminate use of IP holding companies in these havens. But unilateral adoption of a formulary approach would require the United States to renegotiate dozens of tax treaties, and may in any case be susceptible to abuse. One thing is certain: tax reforms that lower tax rates would reduce government's revenue loss from profit shifting. And in fact this has been a major motivation for the wave of rate reductions around the world.

Pass-Through Entities

Do-It-Yourself Tax Reform

In the last chapter, we learned how America's largest corporations are help-ing themselves to tax cuts by shifting profits offshore. In this chapter, we'll see how the corporate tax is being shrunk at the other end. More and more of America's small and midsize businesses have organized their affairs so they are entirely and forever free of the corporate tax.

Businesses subject to the corporate tax are C corporations. There are three no-corporate-tax alternatives: S corporations, partnerships, and sole proprietorships. Collectively, these three tax classifications are referred to as "flow-through" or "pass-through" entities because, unlike C corporations where profits can be bottled up until they are distributed, the profits of these businesses are passed through immediately to owners who must re-port this income on their individual tax returns.

The share of total business activity taking place in pass-through entities has risen significantly over the last three decades. As shown in Table 10-1, pass-through entities accounted for 83 percent of all business returns in 1980. By 2008 that figure had increased to 94 percent. Their share of total receipts, only 13 percent in 1980, grew to 35 percent by 2008. Their share of profits grew from 22 to 49 percent.

Table 10-1. Business Shares by Filing Status, 1980–2008

	1980	1990	2000	2008
S Corporations				
Returns	4%	8%	11%	13%
Receipts	3%	13%	15%	18%
Net income	1%	9%	17%	15%
Partnerships				
Returns	11%	8%	8%	10%
Receipts	4%	4%	9%	14%
Net income	3%	4%	22%	22%
Sole Proprietorships				
Returns	69%	74%	72%	72%
Receipts	6%	6%	4%	4%
Net income	18%	30%	18%	12%
All Pass-Through Businesses (Sum of Above)				
Returns	83%	89%	91%	94%
Receipts	13%	23%	29%	35%
Net income	22%	43%	57%	49%
C Corporations				
Returns	17%	11%	9%	6%
Receipts	87%	77%	71%	65%
Net income	78%	57%	43%	51%

Source: IRS, Statistics of Income.

In 1994, there were 2.3 million Subchapter C corporations subject to the corporate tax. By 2008 the number had shrunk to 1.8 million. Because mostly smaller businesses are switching from Subchapter C to pass-through status, large corporations account for an increasing share of corporate tax revenue. In 1994, the top 1,500 corporations paid 70 percent of corporate tax revenue. In 2008 it only took the top 600 corporations to account for 70 percent of corporate tax revenue.

Because the corporate tax is being hollowed out from below, it is more than ever a tax on big business. This development is the result of two phenomena: the dramatic increase of Subchapter S corporations and the surge, mostly in the 1990s, in the number of limited liability partnerships (LLPs) and limited liability companies (LLCs).

Subchapter S: Sweet Spot for Smaller Businesses

Subchapter S of the Internal Revenue Code was enacted into law in 1958. At the time, there was growing concern that big corporations were becoming too dominant in the American economy. The intent of Subchapter S was to strengthen America's small and family-owned businesses. Subchapter S corporations could have the best of both worlds: the legal privileges of a corporation—limited liability, free transferability of shares, unlimited life—without paying any corporate tax. From the perspective of state law, Subchapter S corporations are no different than other corporations. "Subchapter S" is a tax-filing status, not a separate type of legal entity.

Subchapter S corporations are essentially taxed liked partnerships. Under the original statute, if a corporation had 15 or fewer shareholders, and those shareholders were individuals and U.S. residents, the profits of the corporation would not be subject to corporate tax. Instead, those profits would flow through and immediately be subject to tax on the owners' individual tax returns. In addition to eliminating the double tax on profits, flow-through treatment provided an additional benefit. It allowed shareholders of start-up S corporations to deduct business losses on their individual returns.

The allowable maximum number of S corporation shareholders was increased to 35 in 1982, to 75 in 1996, and to 100 in 2005. For most S corporations, the limitation on the number of shareholders is not an issue. In 2008, S corporations with three or fewer shareholders accounted for 95 percent of S corporation returns.

The dramatic rise popularity of Subchapter S status is shown in Figure 10-1. There were half a million S corporation returns filed in 1980. That number rose to 1.6 million in 1990, 2.9 million in 2000, and 4 million in 2008. As was shown in Table 10-1, profits of Subchapter S corporations in 1980 equaled just 1 percent of all business profits. In 2008 the figure was 15 percent.

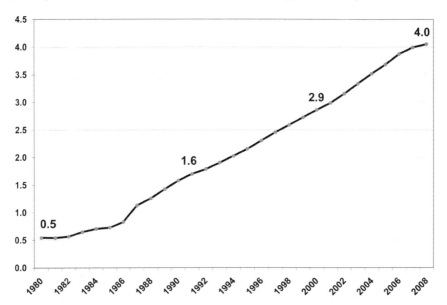

Figure 10-1. The fantastic growth of S corporations, 1980–2008 (in millions). Source: IRS, Statistics of Income.

Traditional Partnerships Give Way to LLPs

The role of partnerships has also grown rapidly over the last three decades. Their share of total business profits has risen from 3 percent in the 1980s to 22 percent in 2008. This increase is almost entirely due to the sky-rocketing growth of two new forms of business organization: the LLP and the closely related LLC.

Both LLPs and LLCs are creatures of state laws. They give non-corporate business owners liability protection comparable to corporate shareholders. For tax purposes, LLPs and LLCs are generally classified as partnerships. Requirements vary from state to state, but, speaking in the most general terms, professional firms practicing law, accounting, and medicine are frequently organized as LLPs, and other lines of business form LLCs. For the purposes of this book, there are few practical differences between the two, and for simplicity's sake we will refer to both as LLPs.

In the early 1980s, LLPs barely existed. Now they are available under the laws of all 50 states and the District of Columbia. Figure 10-2 shows IRS data on businesses filing tax returns as LLPs as well all other partnerships. The "other partnerships" category includes plain-old partnerships with un-limited liability. And it also includes limited partnerships (different from LLPs), where some partners have limited liability and some (general part-ners) have unlimited liability. The first year the IRS collected data on LLPs was in 1993. About 20,000 existed at the time, compared to 1.45 million other partnerships. Subsequently, while other partnerships slowly declined, LLPs grew rapidly in numbers—from 720,000 in 2000 to 1.9 million in 2008.

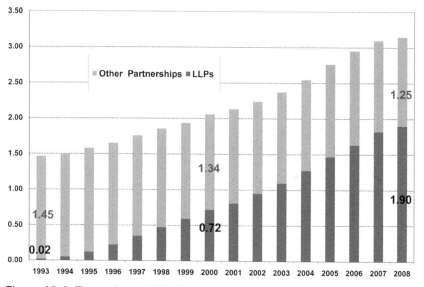

Figure 10-2. The rapid rise of LLPs. Source: IRS, Statistics of Income.

Subchapter S corporations and LLPs both share the essential features of lim-ited liability and freedom from corporation tax. The choice between the two is determined by other considerations. For example, midsize businesses may find LLPs more attractive than S corporations because as LLPs they can have more than 100 owners. In addition, unlike S corporations, LLPs can be owned by foreigners and corporations. For small businesses, LLPs can be more attractive than Subchapter S corporations because state-law filing re-quirements may be less burdensome and less costly.

Sole Proprietorships: Mom-and-Pops and Consultants

A sole proprietorship is the designation the IRS gives to any individual (or married couple filing jointly) who reports business income on Schedule C of Form 1040. In the days of old, this is how your traditional mom-and-pop business might report business profits to the IRS. It was simple and it avoided the double tax burden of the corporate tax.

When it comes to sheer numbers, you can't beat sole proprietorships. There were 22.6 million in 2008. There are twice as many sole proprietorships as there are corporations and partnerships combined. Approximately one out of every six individual tax returns filed includes sole proprietorship income. Figure 10-3 shows that instead of becoming obsolescent, sole proprietorships have grown steadily in every year from 1980 to 2007. Only the great recession of 2008 was able to buck the trend. The growth from 9 to 23 million sole proprietorships has occurred despite the simultaneous increase in the use of Subchapter S organizations with one owner. In 2008 there were 2.4 million Subchapter S corporations with one shareholder.

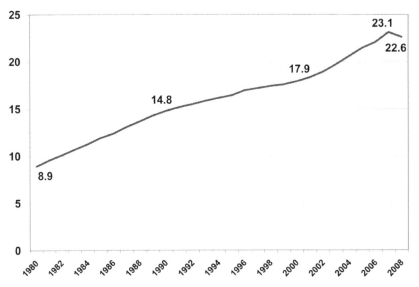

Figure 10-3. Sole proprietorships, 1980–2009 (in millions). Source: IRS, Statistics of Income.

What factors explain this growth? With injury lawyers everywhere, you might wonder why any small business owner would not seek to protect personal assets by incorporating under state law and continue avoiding corporate tax using Subchapter S.

The staying power of sole proprietorships might be explained at least in part by increased compliance by small businesses and service providers who previously worked "off the books" and now report their income to the IRS. But this is only speculation, as no data is available.

Another explanation is that some sole proprietorships are in fact able to get limited liability protection. Many states allow businesses with one owner to form LLCs. The number of LLCs that file as sole proprietorships grew from 126,000 in 2001 to 843,000 in 2008. But this represents less than one-fifth of the increase in sole proprietorships over that period.

More likely, the staying power of sole proprietorship tax filing is the result of fundamental changes in the American economy and in the legal relationships between employers and workers. Figure 10-4 shows that, adjusted for inflation, the size of the average sole proprietorship has been cut in half between 1980 and 2008. Small businesses are getting smaller. This is probably due to as an increase in self-employed consultants, an increase in the number of workers formally classified as "independent contractors," and increase in access to high-speed Internet, which allows almost anybody to become an entrepreneur overnight.

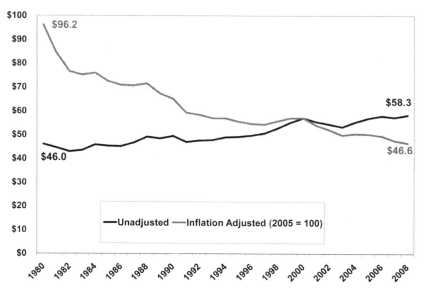

Figure 10-4. Average receipts of sole proprietorships, 1980–2009, in thousands. Source: IRS, Statistics of Income.

Not Such Small Business After All

The essence of reform is getting rid of loopholes—hopefully to pay for lower tax rates. There is no better corporate tax loophole than complete exemption from corporate tax. Small businesses get this tax break because of America's veneration of small business. But not all pass-through entities are small businesses.

Tables 10-2 and 10-3 show the extent to which large businesses entirely escape the corporate tax. In 2008 there were 14,000 S corporations with more than $50 million in receipts. They accounted for 29 percent of all S corporation profit. Their average level of profit was $6.4 million. Other IRS data (not shown in Table 10-2) indicates that over 8 percent of Subchapter S corporation profits were earned by businesses with over $250 million in assets.

Table 10-2. Subchapter S Corporations with $50 Million or More in Receipts, 2008

	Number	Total Profit (Billions)	Average Profit (Millions)	Percentage of Total (All Size) S Corporation Profit
All Industries	14,192	$90.7	$6.4	29%
Agriculture and forestry	147	$0.7	$4.7	25%
Mining	122	$3.9	$31.9	28%
Utilities	25	$0.4	$14.3	58%
Construction	2,201	$13.1	$6.0	36%
Manufacturing	2,363	$20.0	$8.5	47%
Wholesale and retail trade	7,031	$24.0	$3.4	44%
Transportation and warehousing	405	$1.7	$4.1	23%
Information	148	$2.3	$15.6	44%
Finance and insurance	153	$7.1	$46.4	23%
Real estate, rental, and leasing	81	$0.3	$4.2	3%
Professional and technical services	515	$6.5	$12.6	13%

	Number	Total Profit (Billions)	Average Profit (Millions)	Percentage of Total (All Size) S Corporation Profit
Holding companies	95	$4.6	$48.9	72%
Administrative and support services	450	$3.2	$7.1	26%
Educational services	32	$0.5	$16.0	19%
Health care and social assistance	192	$0.8	$4.2	3%
Arts, entertainment, and recreation	76	$0.8	$10.5	22%
Accommodation and food services	115	$0.5	$4.2	13%
Other services	39	$0.3	$8.5	5%

Source: IRS, Statistics of Income.

In 2008 the IRS received 3.1 million partnership returns. Only about 18,000 of those returns, 0.6 percent of the total, had assets of $100 million more. But these partnerships—with an average of 300 partners—accounted for 64 percent of the profits of all partnerships. Average profit for this group was $16.2 million.

There is no obvious dividing line between small and large businesses. It is all a matter of judgment. Nevertheless, the data from Tables 10-2 and 10-3 indicates that a significant portion of the relief from double taxation accrues to businesses that are large by anybody's definition.

Table 10-3. Partnerships with $100 Million or More in Assets, 2008

	Number	Average Number of Partners	Total Profit (Billions)	Average Profit (Millions)	Percentage of Total (All Size) Partnership Profit
All Types	18,180	300	$294.3	$16.2	64%
By Legal Form					
LLP	6,899	82	$27.9	$4.0	51%
Other	11,281	434	$266.4	$23.6	66%
By Broad Industry Class					
Finance	9,884	222	$146.8	$14.9	67%
Real estate	4,403	116	$1.2	$0.3	29%
Other	3,893	708	$146.2	$37.6	62%

Source: IRS, Statistics of Income.

What should be the dividing line between businesses subject to corporate tax and those not? That's not an easy question to answer given that there is no economic justification for the corporation tax in the first place. Economic theory suggests that if there must be a second layer of tax on business, all business income should be subject to the tax. As a practical matter, this is not possible because of America's veneration of small business. Given that immutable political constraint, we should probably at least try for consistency: we should not allow some large businesses to avoid paying taxes while most large business must.

In its list of possible tax reform options, the president's Economic Recovery Advisory Board in 2010 included proposals that would require publicly traded partnerships to pay corporate taxes, and would require businesses above a certain size to be subject to corporate tax. And in mid-2011, rumors abounded that the Treasury Department was considering a proposal that would impose corporate tax on all businesses with more than $50 million of receipts. Proposals like these are likely to remain on the table as long as tax reform and deficit reduction are getting serious consideration.

Summary

One of the most difficult political hurdles for corporate tax reform is its potentially negative effect on pass-through businesses. For example, if deductions and credits *for all business* are used to pay for rate reductions *on corporations*, the opposition of pass-through businesses—including the hugely influential small-business lobby—would be absolute. And when it comes to proposals that entirely eliminate the corporate tax (discussed in Chapters 13 and 14), they often include new taxes that subject pass-through entities to new tax burdens. Carried away by their enthusiasm for a level economic playing field, tax reformers tend to gloss over this issue. But it is a sure bet that any tax reform plan that has a real chance of becoming law will have to grapple with this issue front-and-center.

State Corporate Taxes

Making a Bad Situation Worse

At the federal level, the corporate tax is our most complex and economically damaging tax. State corporation taxes take this bad situation and make it worse. To collect their corporate tax, each state starts with the federal corporate tax and then makes adjustments and modifications to meet its own set of policy and revenue objectives. Then each must engage in the always contentious fight with corporations about what share of national profits falls inside its jurisdiction. For all this aggravation—for all this fingernail-scratching-on-the-blackboard pain—the states collectively never raise more than one-third of the revenue that the IRS collects from the federal corporate tax—and in some years considerably less.

Forty-two states and the District of Columbia have full-fledged corporation taxes. Four have broad-based business taxes that in varying degrees take the place of corporation taxes. (Two of the four are classified as corporation taxes by the Census Bureau.) And the four remaining states have no corporate or general business tax at all. In 2009 the Census Bureau tallied a grand total of $40.5 billion in state corporate tax revenues.

The corporation tax is not a major source of revenue for most states. Individual income taxes and sales taxes are far more important. Nationwide, corporate tax accounts for 3.6 percent of total state revenues. Table 11-1 shows that in only six states does the corporate tax (or a general business tax) account for more than 5 percent of total state revenue: New Hampshire (8.7%), California (8.4%), Wisconsin (7.8%), Alaska (7.1%), Illinois (6.8%), and New Jersey (5.8%). Nearly one-quarter of all state corporation tax is collected by the state of California.

Table 11-1. State Corporation Taxes, Rates, and Revenue

Jurisdiction	Top Corporate Rate (2011)	Corporate Tax Revenue (Millions) (2009)	Corporate Tax As a Percentage of Total State Revenue (2009)
United States	--	$40,478	3.6%
Alabama	6.50%	$494	2.3%
Alaska	9.40%	$632	7.1%
Arizona	6.97%	$592	2.5%
Arkansas	6.50%	$346	2.7%
California	8.84%	$9,536	8.4%
Colorado	4.63%	$330	3.2%
Connecticut	7.50%	$444	2.0%
Delaware	8.70%	$209	3.6%
District of Columbia	9.98%	$420	3.6%
Florida	5.50%	$1,837	4.0%
Georgia	6.00%	$695	2.1%
Hawaii	6.40%	$79	1.2%
Idaho	7.60%	$142	2.6%
Illinois	9.50%	$2,752	6.8%
Indiana	8.50%	$839	3.0%
Iowa	12.00%	$264	2.0%

Jurisdiction	Top Corporate Rate (2011)	Corporate Tax Revenue (Millions) (2009)	Corporate Tax As a Percentage of Total State Revenue (2009)
Kansas	4.00%	$371	3.2%
Kentucky	6.00%	$390	2.0%
Louisiana	8.00%	$613	2.7%
Maine	8.93%	$143	2.2%
Maryland	8.25%	$749	3.1%
Massachusetts	8.25%	$1,790	4.8%
Michigan	Business Tax (4.95%)	$703	1.5%
Minnesota	9.80%	$779	3.4%
Mississippi	5.00%	$324	2.3%
Missouri	6.25%	$279	1.5%
Montana	6.75%	$164	3.4%
Nebraska	7.81%	$198	2.7%
Nevada	No corporate tax	--	0.0%
New Hampshire	Business Profits Tax (8.5%)	$ 493	8.7%
New Jersey	9.00%	$2,529	5.8%
New Mexico	7.60%	$204	2.1%
New York	7.10%	$4,428	4.8%
North Carolina	6.90%	$901	2.9%
North Dakota	6.40%	$130	3.0%
Ohio	Commercial Activities Tax (0.26%)	$521	2.1%

Jurisdiction	Top Corporate Rate (2011)	Corporate Tax Revenue (Millions) (2009)	Corporate Tax As a Percentage of Total State Revenue (2009)
Oklahoma	6.00%	$343	2.0%
Oregon	7.60%	$259	3.3%
Pennsylvania	9.99%	$1,741	4.5%
Rhode Island	9.00%	$108	2.3%
South Carolina	5.00%	$219	1.1%
South Dakota	No corporate tax	$49	2.0%
Tennessee	6.50%	$816	4.4%
Texas	Margin Tax (1%)	--	0.0%
Utah	5.00%	$246	2.8%
Vermont	8.50%	$87	1.9%
Virginia	6.00%	$633	2.4%
Washington	No corporate tax	--	0.0%
West Virginia	8.50%	$421	3.8%
Wisconsin	7.90%	$657	7.8%
Wyoming	No corporate tax	--	0.0%

Source: U.S. Census Bureau and the Tax Foundation.

The heyday of state corporate taxation was the 1980s, when tax revenue averaged 7.6 percent of corporate profits. In the 1990s, the average declined to 5.4 percent. And since then the average has been 4.1 percent. This decline, illustrated in Figure 11-1, is due to a combination of legislative relief and aggressive tax planning.

Figure 11-1. State corporation taxes as a share of U.S. domestic profits, 1948–2009. Source: U.S. Census Bureau and Bureau of Economic Analysis.

State corporate taxes may be down, but they are not out. State budgets have been extremely tight as a result of the recession. And unlike the federal government, states cannot borrow to meet their general revenue needs. It will not be easy for any state to forgo the revenues it gets from business taxes. For example, despite a Republican legislative majority, Republican governor Nikki Haley of South Carolina was unable to win passage in the 2011 legislative session of her August 2010 campaign proposal to repeal the state's corporate income tax.

Trench Warfare

Businesses and state tax collectors are engaged in an endless battle over the corporate tax. State legislators cannot seem to make up their minds who to side with—one year wishing to collect more revenue, the next wishing to provide incentives. The results is an uncertain and ever-changing corporate tax landscape where the amount of effort expended administering and complying with the tax is out of proportion with the revenue collected. In addition to the usual fights over tax rates and targeted tax breaks that we see at the federal level, state corporation taxes have their own special set of convoluted controversies. The following paragraphs describe three of them.

First there is the issue of *nexus*. This term refers to the level and nature of business activity that a corporation must have in a state before the state can impose tax. Obviously, if a corporation has a manufacturing facility inside a state's border, the corporation will be liable for the state's corporation tax. But what about delivery of products to a neighboring state? Does that second jurisdiction have nexus? Does it matter if the corporation uses its own trucks? Does it matter if those trucks are garaged and repaired by the corporation in the neighboring state? Does the presence of a sales force in the neighboring state establish nexus? These are not easy questions to answer. And each state has its own set of rules. Businesses have accused the states of trying to "export" taxes to out-of-state businesses and repeatedly have tried to get Congress to require states to use a limited and uniform nexus standard. (And yes, Congress does have the constitutional authority to restrict the ways states collect taxes.)

The second issue is what is known as *combined reporting*. Many states allow profits to be attributed to out-of-state subsidiaries even when those subsidiaries are closely associated with in-state business. This loophole makes it possible for corporations to shift profits from high-tax states to low-tax states and to no-tax out-of-state holding companies. The most prominent example of the abuse made possible by a lack of combined reporting is the sequestration of valuable trademarks into Delaware holding companies. These companies charge parent companies royalties for the use of these trademarks, reducing profits in the states where the companies really do business. About half the states with corporation taxes have combined reporting. Legislators wishing to increase revenue continuously advocate for combined reporting, while legislators wishing to improve competitiveness of in-state businesses fight against it.

The third area of controversy is formulary *apportionment*. In the 1950s, under the threat of action by the federal government, most of the states agreed to a three-factor formula for apportioning profits for purposes of imposing corporate tax. Under this system, a state's share of a corporation's taxable profits was equal to the average of the state's share of the corporation's nationwide sales, property, and payroll. Over the past two decades, states have been moving away from the equal-weighting of the three factors to increased weighting of sales. Some states have gone to the limit and only use sales. This trend reduces taxes on in-state producers at the expense of companies "importing" products into the state. Besides the political advantages, this change encourages in-state job creation because taxes on in-state investment and employment are cut.

Possible Reforms of State Taxes

State corporation taxes contribute greatly to the non-uniform treatment of businesses within the United States. State corporate tax rates vary. State definitions of taxable corporate profits vary. State definitions of taxable corporate entities vary. State formulas for apportioning the profits of multistate businesses vary. On top of all this, states are keen to provide special corporate tax incentives on a case-by-case basis—along with property and sales tax incentives and other forms of aid—to businesses threatening to move out of or on the verge of moving into their jurisdictions. All of the resulting complexity and efficiency-draining distortions reduce national competitiveness.

One way to eliminate most of the complexity and controversy surrounding state corporate taxes would be to require states that wish to impose a corporation tax to use the federal corporate tax base, allow the IRS to administer the tax, and then apportion taxable corporate income of multistate businesses under a uniform set of rules. This approach does not eliminate tax competition because states could still bid against each other by choosing whatever tax rate they wish. This approach would be similar to what has been adopted in Canada. It is also similar to the common consolidated corporate tax base now being considered by the European Union to replace its member states' corporate taxes.

There are two paths for achieving this reform. States could enter into negotiations under the auspices of some public-spirited, nonpartisan institution and voluntarily agree to a uniform add-on tax. Unfortunately, states instinctively cling to their sovereignty like a dog clings to a bone. States are reluctant to give up any of their taxing authority. They will never agree to coordination unless under strong coercion (as they were in the 1950s when they moved toward uniform apportionment formulas).

The only viable path is the second alternative: congressional action. Under the Constitution, Congress has the power to affirmatively regulate state taxing power. But there is no interest in Congress for this type of reform. Business groups like the current system. The extra complexity is worth it to them because the pressure is always on states to provide more loopholes. With business and the state governments opposed, Congress has no political motivation for change.

If fundamental tax reform were ever to occur at the federal level, it could be a catalyst for change at the state level. For example, there is a lot of discussion of replacing the current corporate tax with some sort of value-added tax or of replacing all federal income taxes with a flat tax. (We'll discuss these options more in Chapters 13 and 14.) States currently collecting corporate tax depend heavily on federal rules and enforcement efforts. Because it would be extremely difficult for states to continue corporate taxation if the federal corporate tax were repealed, states would almost certainly have to move in parallel with the federal government. Whatever the federal replacement for the corporate tax might be, that would be the new starting point for determining state business taxes.

Some states have already replaced or are considering replacing their corporation taxes with entirely new business taxes. In 2005, Ohio repealed its corporate tax and replaced it with a 0.26 percent tax on gross business receipts, known as the Commercial Activity Tax (CAT). This tax applies to all businesses, not just corporations. This change by Ohio will help Ohio manufacturers by redistributing the business tax burden to retailers, wholesalers, and service firms. It is certainly simpler than the corporate tax. However, the tax is unfairly and unevenly applied from the perspective of the consumer. Goods that go through many intermediate stages of production and delivery by different firms may be subject to much higher cumulative levels of tax than goods that are built from scratch and delivered to a customer by a single firm.

Beginning in 2008, Texas stopped collecting corporate tax. It now has what is called the Texas Margin Tax. This tax applies to all businesses, not just corporations. The tax rate is 1 percent for most businesses and 0.5 percent for wholesalers and retailers. Under the new law, the "margin" subject to tax is the lesser of (1) total revenue minus cost of goods sold, (2) total revenue times 70 percent, or (3) total revenue minus employee compensation. The first of these means the business is effectively subject to a value-added tax. The second of these options means the business is effectively subject to a gross receipts tax. The third option is not like anything in any tax textbook, but serves the important political purpose of reducing the burden on labor-intensive service-oriented businesses—like law and accounting firms—that may never have been subject to a general business tax before.

California still has a corporate tax, but reform proposals have received some attention. In 2010, at the end of his administration, former Governor Arnold Schwarzenegger endorsed a sweeping reform plan that included a new Net Business Receipts Tax. Under the proposal, all businesses, not just corporations, would pay a tax on the difference between their gross receipts and their purchases from other businesses. There would be no deductions for wages or interest. Essentially, the new tax would be a value-added tax. The revenues from the new tax would be used to eliminate the state corporation income tax, dramatically cut the state sales tax rate, and flatten the progressive rate structure of the income tax. The tax got no-where in the legislature. Conservatives opposed a new tax on business. Liberals opposed the tax because they believed the burden would fall disproportionately on the poor.

Summary

The complexity and issues with the federal corporation tax are so over-whelming that it is tempting to dismiss state corporate taxes as relatively unimportant. But the problems cannot be ignored. Our current tangled web of state corporation taxes is antithetical to the goals of simplicity, fairness, and efficiency. If we wish to truly reform corporate taxes in the United States, fundamental changes to state corporation taxes must be included. Unfortunately, politics and tight budgets keep prospects of a widespread state corporate tax cleanup extremely remote.

Corporate Tax Simplification
Always the Bridesmaid

Paying tolls on a crowded highway is nobody's idea of a good time. Economists analyzing the phenomenon will tell you tolls impose three separate costs on drivers. First, there is the monetary cost of paying the toll itself. Second, there are the efficiency costs on drivers who take slower and less direct back roads to avoid paying the toll. Third, for drivers who do not take the back roads, there are the burdens involved in the process of paying the toll: out-of-pocket costs (e.g., extra gasoline used idling), the hassles (e.g., whining kids, bumper-to-bumper traffic), and the time wasted waiting in line.

Taxes, like tolls, impose these same three types of costs. First, taxpayers have the monetary costs of the taxes themselves. Second, there are the efficiency costs that stem from taxpayers' changing their behavior to minimize tax. Third, there are the out-of-pocket costs, the anxiety, and the time involved in the process of paying the tax. This chapter is about the third of those three costs—the compliance costs—as they relate to corporate taxes.

Tax Complexity in General

Somewhere out there are people who are organized, public-spirited math wizards not intimidated by bureaucratic rules. And then there are the rest of us.

For most Americans, the annual ritual of paying income taxes is misery. There is the cost in time and money of recordkeeping, reading instructions, filling out forms, and meeting deadlines. And then, if you think you might qualify for one of those tax breaks politicians like to advertise, congratulations! That involves more forms and instructions. There is the anxiety of making a mistake and being audited. And just when you are starting to feel a little relieved as you wind up your filing obligations to Uncle Sam, most of us have to repeat the exercise to pay state income taxes. TurboTax and other tax software have done a lot to smooth out the rough spots. But still, for most Americans, the words "April 15th" are more dreaded than "root canal" or "we have to call the plumber."

Small businesses experience the same pain multiplied a dozen times. They are not big enough to have their own in-house staff, but they face far more tax complexity than the average individual taxpayer. Business compliance costs are, adjusted for size, higher for small business than for large business. And as with individuals, the intangible anxiety costs are extremely high. Small businesses are often struggling financially and taxes could put them over the edge. Expert and confident in their fields of specialization, small business owners are intimidated and frustrated by seemingly endless and undecipherable requirements for complying with tax rules.

Economists have tried to measure the compliance cost of taxation on the American public, but it is an extremely difficult task. There is a lot of variation in costs across different types of taxpayers. A single individual with one job and one bank account should have little difficulty. For a wealthy couple with a small business and a diversified portfolio, it is an entirely different story. Furthermore, very few of us really can make an accurate assessment of time spent complying with the tax law. With those caveats in mind, a reasonable ballpark estimate for the total cost of compliance for the economy, based on a review of the available estimates, might be about 1 percent of GDP—about $150 billion. That works out to an average of about $450 for every individual in the United States.

The IRS estimates that Americans spend a total of 6.1 billion hours each year complying with federal taxes. To arrive at this figure, the IRS multiplies the number of forms filed by the estimated average time it takes to complete the form. That's equivalent to the full-time employment of 3 million workers. If you paid those workers approximately $25 an hour, you arrive at the 1 percent of GDP figure discussed above. Some analysts—especially anti-tax conservatives—estimate the figure to be double or triple that amount. They could be right. Nobody really knows. All estimates of compliance costs are nothing more than educated guesswork.

Corporate Tax Complexity

What portion of those costs is related to the corporation tax? Most of the hours attributed to tax compliance are related to the taxation of individuals, sole proprietorships, partnerships, and Subchapter S corporations. Also included in the overall total are the compliance costs associated with employment taxes, estate and gift taxes, and excise taxes.

If the IRS methodology is to be believed, only a small fraction of total compliance costs is related to C corporations. In 2008, approximately 1.8 million C corporation returns were filed. Estimated average time to complete the return was 194 hours. Multiplying the two figures yields total time spent on corporate taxes equal to 350 million hours—about 6 percent of the estimated 6.1-billion-hour total. If the average cost of corporate labor is $50 an hour, the compliance cost would be $17.5 billion annually.

A 2002 study sponsored by the IRS that used survey results estimated that midsize and large businesses incurred compliance costs of approximately $22 billion in 1999. Adjusted for economic growth, that figure would be approximately $34 billion in 2008. About three-quarters of all business receipts from businesses with over $100 million in assets are from C corporations. So another estimate of C corporation compliance cost is three-quarters of $34 billion, or about $25 billion.

Again, as with overall tax compliance costs, any estimates of compliance costs relating to the federal corporate tax are speculative. One problem is that it is difficult to separate the costs of financial accounting and planning from the costs of tax accounting and planning. Another problem is separating corporate tax compliance costs from other tax compliance costs. All big corporations have tax departments, but a lot of their time is spent working on other taxes, including property taxes, payroll taxes, and excise taxes. Third, a lot of corporate tax compliance cost is not related to the U.S. federal corporate tax. General Electric pointed out in its latest annual report that it filed over 6,400 income tax returns in over 250 global taxing jurisdictions, and that the company is under examination or engaged in tax litigation in many of these jurisdictions. A fourth problem is that not all compliance costs are incurred by the tax department. For example, an IRS audit involving transfer-pricing issues will involve managers from all parts of the organization.

Sources of Complexity

We will never arrive at a precise figure for corporate compliance costs, but we can be certain it is large. Time is better spent in figuring out where the complexity exists and what can be done to reduce it. The following three examples illustrate some of the problems.

Corporate Alternative Minimum Tax

The purpose of the corporate alternative minimum tax (AMT), like the individual alternative minimum tax, is to prevent any taxpayer from getting so many tax benefits that no tax is paid at all. Yes, Congress likes to shell out tax benefits, but it is bad press when anybody is "zeroing out"—especially large, profitable corporations.

To avoid this problem, Congress requires corporations with over $7.5 million of gross receipts to check and see if they are liable for AMT. To calculate AMT, corporations start with regular taxable income and then enlarge that figure by removing certain tax benefits. AMT income is then multiplied by the 20 percent AMT rate. To the extent the new AMT number exceeds regular corporate tax, the corporations owe AMT. So after a corporation computes its regular corporate tax, it must compute a second tax liability using a different set of rules. The corporate AMT is an accounting and administrative nightmare.

In most cases, the AMT is a temporary tax. That's because AMT liability can be credited against future regular tax liability. Here is an example of how it works. Suppose every year in the past a corporation computed an AMT of $30 million and a regular corporate tax of $35 million. No AMT was ever due. Then, in the current year, AMT jumps to $37 million. There is AMT liability of $2 million in the current year. In the next year the corporation returns to its usual pattern. It has $35 million of regular tax and $2 million of AMT credits. Net tax payment in the next year is $33 million. Over all the years, regular corporate tax averages $35 million, and average AMT is zero.

Despite all this mumbo jumbo, the AMT has not been effective in eliminating the unsightly phenomenon of large, profitable corporations paying little or no tax. This is because the tax breaks (called "preferences") used to calculate AMT are a small subset of tax benefits available to corporations. The real culprits behind big low-tax corporations—high levels of corporate debt, aggressive transfer pricing, accelerated depreciation, and tax shelters—are not caught by the AMT. The corporate AMT is a toothless tiger.

Not only does the corporate AMT fail to serve its original purpose, it only raises a relatively small amount of revenue. Table 12-1 shows AMT payments and net AMT revenue raised after credits for the years 1987 through 2008. In many years, AMT credits against regular tax have exceeded AMT liability, making the AMT an overall revenue loser. Over 22 years, the corporate AMT has raised a total of only $13 billion. Although corporate tax reformers are desperately searching for revenues to pay for rate reduction, their proposals usually also include elimination of the corporate AMT. This is one of the most obvious ways of simplifying the corporate tax.

Table 12-1. Corporate AMT Revenues, 1987–2008 (in Billions)

Year	AMT Payments	AMT Credits Used	Net AMT Revenue (After Credits)
1987	2.2		2.2
1988	3.4	0.5	2.9
1989	3.5	0.8	2.7
1990	8.1	0.7	7.4
1991	5.3	1.5	3.8
1992	4.9	2.3	2.6
1993	4.9	3.0	1.9
1994	4.5	3.3	1.2
1995	4.3	4.8	−0.5
1996	3.8	4.7	−0.9
1997	3.9	4.1	−0.2
1998	3.3	3.4	−0.1
1999	3.0	3.5	−0.5
2000	3.9	5.2	−1.3
2001	1.8	3.3	−1.5
2002	2.5	2.0	0.5
2003	2.3	3.4	−1.1
2004	3.4	3.7	−0.3
2005	3.3	7.1	−3.8
2006	3.7	5.9	−2.2

Year	AMT Payments	AMT Credits Used	Net AMT Revenue (After Credits)
2007	3.2	3.2	0.0
2008	2.3	1.9	0.4
Sum	81.6	68.3	13.3

Source: IRS, Statistics of Income.

Taxation of Foreign Profits

Another major source of complexity for large corporations are U.S. tax rules for taxing foreign profits. It is generally agreed that U.S. rules for multinational taxation are more complicated than the rules of other countries. Still, although a lot can be done to simplify these rules, much of the complexity is unavoidable.

You might think that completely exempting foreign profits of U.S. corporations (a so-called "territorial" system, discussed in Chapter 8) from U.S. tax would do wonders for complexity. After all, what could be simpler than collecting zero tax? Well, it turns out that many of the complex rules would remain, and some might have to be strengthened. Disputes would continue to rage between multinationals and the IRS over transfer pricing and other issues concerning the location of income and expenses. To protect the U.S. tax base, foreign profits from passive investment must continue to be subject to U.S. tax. And now that foreign profits would be eligible for exemption instead of just deferral from U.S. tax, complex anti-deferral rules designed to prevent abuse would become anti-exemption rules.

There is one area of international taxation that would enjoy considerable simplification under a territorial system. Foreign tax credit rules would no longer be needed for exempt income. Moreover, the huge hassle U.S. multinationals face trying to match dividend repatriations to those available for foreign tax credits would become a welcome relic of the past.

The Research Credit

Not all complexity in the tax law is foisted on corporations by a money-hungry Congress. Sometimes they ask for it. And there is perhaps no better example of this than the immensely popular tax credit for research activities.

As pointed out in Chapter 6, there are three alternative methods of computing the credit. Two of these options are incremental credits in which the credit rate is a function of the difference between current expenditures and prior years' expenditures. This means that calculation of the credit requires information from multiple past years, as well the current year. Sometimes that recordkeeping must extend back to the 1980s. If there have been any mergers and acquisitions between the current year and so-called base years, complex adjustments must be made. Start-up companies have their own complex set of rules.

Further problems arise due to the inherent difficulty in defining qualified research expenditures. There is a running battle between the IRS and industry about the definition of qualified research. The statute seems to say that in order to qualify, research should involve the discovery of new information. But under intense pressure from corporations, that requirement has been dropped. Then there is the question of expenditures on different types of personnel. Of course, scientists working in labs should qualify. But what about supervisors, administrators, and sales personnel, who are also in involved in research? Research is not easy to quantify and there will never be a bright line separating qualified research from nonqualified.

The Prospect for Corporate Tax Simplification

Despite the incessant talk about the need for tax simplification, Congress and the IRS are rarely able to make inroads. The need to prevent abuse, to be accurate, to be fair, to deliver benefits through the tax system, and to reach political compromise almost always take precedence. All the major proponents of the Tax Reform Act of 1986 wanted to simplify the tax law. They failed miserably. The 1986 act added vast new complexity to the tax law. And since 1986, the tax law has become even more complex.

It is important to distinguish simplification efforts for individuals and small businesses from those for large corporations. The compliance costs for individuals and small business are proportionately larger than they are for large corporations. Furthermore, they have an emotional element—absent from corporate tax compliance—that makes them a hot-button political issue.

Because of the widespread tax anxiety among the populace, any politician can get applause for proposing to simplify the code. This is the appeal of the Flat Tax (discussed in the next chapter) and its promise of a postcard-size tax return. Most efforts by politicians to simplify tax law are overwhelmingly focused on the problems faced by individuals and small business. Corporate tax simplification is purely about dollars and cents. When the posturing and speechmaking are done, simplification is no longer a priority. In the making of corporate tax policy, simplification is often a nice ex-post justification and added talking points in favor of a proposal. And when a popular, new provision coming down the legislative pipeline adds complexity, the concept of tax simplification is simply ignored.

To repeal the corporate AMT, we would have to live in a world where Congress valued simplicity more than revenue. To repeal the research credit, we would have to live in a world where businesses valued simplicity more than they valued billions of tax credits. We don't live in such a world.

And even if we did, there are significant limitations on what even the most radical corporate tax simplification could achieve. As long as states and other countries around the world have corporate taxes, most of the basic headaches of corporate tax remain in place even if somehow the federal corporate tax were to disappear. And here is the real kicker: Switching to a simpler system necessarily adds complexity, as taxpayers must learn new rules and comply with two sets of rules during the transition period. There is nothing simple about simplification.

Summary

Simplification should remain a priority in tax reform. The benefits may be smaller than advertised, and the effort required more arduous than many believe. But it is still worth the effort. Reducing compliance costs by a few billion dollars frees resources and brainpower that can be put to far more productive uses than dodging and weaving from Uncle Sam.

Fundamental Tax Reform

Ready for a Revenue Revolution?

There is conventional tax reform. And then there is fundamental tax reform.

Conventional tax reform involves modifying the current system by lowering tax rates and broadening the tax base. Fundamental tax reform involves getting rid of individual and corporate income taxes entirely and replacing them with a whole new tax system. Conventional tax reform is a gargantuan political task, but it has been done—like manned flight to the moon. Fundamental tax reform in a large economy is entirely unprecedented—like going to Mars.

The two most popular options for fundamental reform ideas are the Flat Tax and the Fair Tax. The Flat Tax would replace the corporate and individual income taxes with a single-rate tax on individuals and businesses. The tax would be so simple that most taxpayers would only need to file a post-card-size return. The most prominent advocates of the Flat Tax are Steve Forbes, millionaire publisher and former candidate for the Republican presidential nomination, and Dick Armey, Republican from Texas and former Majority Leader of the House of Representatives.

The Fair Tax would replace the current tax system with a national sales tax. Individuals would no longer have to file tax returns at all! Former Republican congressman John Linder of Georgia has been the main promoter of the Fair Tax.

Before discussing these fundamental reforms, I will provide an overview of the value-added tax (VAT). This may seen a strange to anybody who is familiar with conservatives' visceral hatred of the VAT, which they view as the funding mechanism that makes possible the extensive social programs in Europe. What does the "liberal" VAT have to do with the "conservative" Flat and Fair Taxes? As we shall see, they are in fact almost economically identical. They are all taxes on consumption.

The critical distinction between existing VATs and proposed fundamental reforms is context. Consumption taxes like VATs so far have been *add-on taxes* appended to the existing income tax system. Consumption taxes like the Flat and Fair Taxes would be *replacement taxes* that would ultimately not increase the overall size of tax collections. Conservative enthusiasm for consumption taxes like the Flat Tax and the Fair Tax would instantly evaporate if they were proposed as add-on taxes.

Value-Added Taxation

Value-added is a measure of business activity. It is the difference between a business's sales revenue and the cost of its purchases from other businesses. In the vertical chain of production and distribution—like that, say, from a wheat farmer to a supermarket selling bread—the sum total of all the value added by each business in the chain equals the retail sales price.

Value-added taxes are collected from businesses. The biggest differences between VATs and corporate taxes are that VATs do not allow deductions for wages and interest and—on the plus side for business—they allow capital to be expensed instead of requiring depreciation. Another difference is that value-added taxes apply to all businesses, corporate and non-corporate (although for administrative simplicity there are often exceptions for the very smallest of businesses). As shown in Table 13-1, VATs are collected by governments of all the world's biggest economies, except the United States.

Table 13-1. VATs Around the World

Country	Year VAT First Implemented	VAT Rate in 2010
Australia	2000	10.0
Canada	1991	5.0
Chile	1975	19.0
China	1994	17.0

Country	Year VAT First Implemented	VAT Rate in 2010
France	1968	19.6
Germany	1968	19.0
Greece	1987	19.0
Hungary	1988	25.0
Ireland	1972	21.0
Italy	1973	20.0
Japan	1989	5.0
Korea	1977	10.0
Mexico	1980	16.0
Netherlands	1969	19.0
New Zealand	1986	12.5
Norway	1970	25.0
Poland	1993	22.0
Portugal	1986	20.0
Spain	1986	16.0
Sweden	1969	25.0
Switzerland	1995	7.6
Turkey	1985	18.0
United Kingdom	1973	17.5
United States	--	None

Source: Organisation for Economic Co-operation and Development

Around the world, the trend seems to be for increasing reliance on value-added taxation. In 2011, the Conservative-led ruling coalition in the United Kingdom raised the VAT rate from 17.5 to 20 percent. And in Japan, highly influential business groups are lobbying for an increase in the VAT from 5 to at least 10 percent.

Value-added taxes are much more favorable than income taxes for saving and investment. The main reason for this is that VATs generally allow businesses an immediate write-off of capital purchases. The value of expensing is so beneficial that economists consider it equivalent to exempting capital income from tax. With income from saving exempt, only consumption is taxed. That's why a VAT is considered a consumption tax.

There are two key features of consumption taxes that drive their economics and the politics. First, consumption taxes do not penalize savings like income taxes do. So replacing the income tax with a consumption tax will increase saving. Increasing saving will increase capital formation, which in turn increases productivity and competitiveness. The main economic justification for replacing an income tax with a consumption tax is the boost it will provide to competitiveness. Although economists argue about the size of the economic benefit, there is widespread agreement that consumption taxation is economically superior to income taxation.

The second important feature of consumption taxation is that it is relatively more burdensome on low-income households than high-income households. That's because poor families typically spend a larger share of their income than do rich families. (For example, a poor family may, by borrowing, spend more than its income, while a rich family may save 20 percent of its income.) And so, all things otherwise kept equal, a switch from income to consumption taxation would shift the burden of taxation down the income scale.

Republicans object to value-added taxation because they see it as a "money machine" for big government. Democrats object to the redistribution of the tax burden to the poor. Pundits quip that Democrats will favor a VAT when they realize it is a money machine and Republicans will support it when they realize it redistributes burden away from high-income households.

No matter what your personal preferences may be, you should acknowledge that if a VAT is ever going to become law in the United States, there will have to be accommodations made to alleviate the burden on low-income families. With the intent of alleviating the burden on the poor, most VAT systems now in place provide preferential treatment for various necessities. Those items typically include home-prepared food, medical care, and some types of clothing. Although it is widely adopted, tax experts consider this bifurcated approach a clumsy and complex solution to the fairness issue. (After all, rich people can purchase large amounts of "necessities" eligible for a reduced VAT rate.)

A preferred alternative among policy experts for the regressivity problem is to provide cash rebates (or refundable tax credits) to low-income households. One novel approach made possible by modern technology would provide tax relief for necessities only to low-income families using "smart cards" to verify their identity.

Before concluding this brief overview of value-added taxation, it is worth taking a moment to discuss the VAT's role in cross-border trade. Most VATs around the world have a feature known as *border adjustability*. By international agreement, VATs are taxes on domestic consumption. That means exports are not subject to tax by the exporting country, and imports are subject to tax as they enter the country. Border-tax adjustments are not available for corporate taxes.

Many politicians consider border-tax adjustability to be a major benefit of value-added taxation. They view border adjustments as subsidies for exports and tariff-like penalties on imports. However, most economists believe that the trade advantages of border adjustments are only an illusion. Border-tax adjustments are necessary to keep a level playing field between imports and domestically produced goods (both taxed at the same rate when there are border adjustments) in each country's home market.

The Flat Tax and the Fair Tax

If somebody could invent a consumption tax that had all the pro-growth benefits without unduly adding extra burden on the poor, it would be a considerable achievement. The Flat Tax is a consumption tax that attempts to do exactly that.

The Flat Tax is a VAT split into two parts. As noted previously, a VAT is a tax imposed exclusively on businesses. A Flat Tax takes some of the VAT business burden and imposes it on individuals. If you recall, a VAT does not allow a deduction for wages. In contrast, the Flat Tax does allow businesses to deduct wages. So, instead of wages being taxed at the business level, as under a VAT, wages are taxed at the individual level under a Flat Tax. To alleviate the burden on low-income families, the Flat Tax grants a large standard deduction—something like $20,000 each year for a family. Table 13-2 shows how, except for the standard deduction, the Flat Tax is equivalent to a VAT.

Table 13-2. The Equivalence of the Flat Tax and the VAT

VAT (20% Rate)		Flat Tax (20% Rate)	
Business Tax		**Business Tax**	
Gross receipts	$100.00	Gross receipts	$100.00
Less		*Less*	
Materials cost	$25.00	Materials cost	$25.00
Capital expenditures	$10.00	Capital expenditures	$10.00
		Employee compensation	$50.00
Total cost	$35.00	Total cost	$85.00
Equals		*Equals*	
Tax base	$65.00	Tax base	$15.00
Tax at 20% rate	$13.00	Tax at 20% rate	$3.00
Individual Tax		**Individual Tax**	
None		Employee compensation	$50.00
		Less	
		Standard deduction	$20.00
		Equals	
		Tax base	$30.00
		Tax at 20% rate	$6.00
Total business and individual tax	$13.00	**Total business and individual tax**	$9.00
		Total tax without standard deduction	$13.00

The Flat Tax has largely the same economic characteristics of any broad-based consumption tax. Because the tax effectively exempts capital income, the bias against capital formation under current law is eliminated. By replacing the current individual income and corporate taxes, the Flat Tax could foster increases in productivity, wages, economic growth, and competitiveness.

By eliminating the corporate tax, the bias in favor of debt over equity would vanish and so would the bias in favor of non-corporate business. These economic benefits, however, could turn into political liabilities. Debt-heavy business would howl in protest unless the rate were sufficiently low. Non-corporate businesses that paid no entity-level tax before now would incur large new federal tax liabilities.

A pure Flat Tax would eliminate all credits and special deductions. But there have been Flat Tax proposals that have allowed the deductions for mortgage interest and charitable contributions to remain. In the real world, any Flat Tax that had a chance of becoming law would probably retain many tax breaks that exist under current law. Even still, the exemption of capital gains, interest, and dividends from individual income tax—eliminating so many hundreds of special tax rules on saving and investment income—would make the new tax system much simpler relative to current law.

Because of the generous standard deduction, the Flat Tax imposes less burden on the poor than a plain-vanilla VAT. But wealthy families still would significantly benefit relative to current law because corporate profits would no longer be double-taxed, the estate and gift taxes would be eliminated, and the progressive rate structure would be flattened. To address the lack of high-end progressicity in the Flat Tax, some have proposed what is called an X-tax. The X-tax essentially has the same structure as the Flat Tax, with the important difference that wages are taxed at progressive rates.

For those who seek to pull the income tax out by its roots, the major competitor to the Flat Tax is the Fair Tax, a national retail sales tax that would replace all existing federal taxes. Congressman Linder first proposed the tax in 1999, and when he left Congress in 2010 his latest version of the bill had over 60 cosponsors. Companion legislation introduced by Senator Saxby Chambliss (R-Georgia) had four cosponsors. *The Fair Tax Book*, coauthored by Linder and radio host Neil Boortz, spent time on top of the *New York Times* bestseller list in 2006.

Like the VAT and the Flat Tax, the Fair Tax is a consumption tax and shares the economics of those taxes. It would help promote economic growth by removing the income and corporate taxes' bias against saving and investment. But it would also redistribute the tax burden from the rich to poor. To partially address this last problem, the Linder plan would provide families cash rebates for the amount of tax that would be paid on purchases equal to poverty-level income.

The Fair Tax plan would eliminate the IRS. The tax would be collected by the states. There is much dispute about the rate needed for a Fair Tax to make up the revenue lost from the repeal of all other federal taxes, but it almost certainly is in the neighborhood of 30 percent. But probably the most damaging critique of the Fair Tax is that it ventures into the no-man's land of tax enforcement. Collecting all revenue at high rates from retailers and service providers could result in widespread tax evasion. The difficulty of enforcing a broad-based sales tax at high rates is often explained to be the reason most nations have adopted the economically equivalent VAT instead of a sales tax.

The Name Game

One word of warning before concluding our discussion of value-added taxation. Many sweeping tax proposals are essentially VATs even though their proponents will never identify them as such. It is political poison—especially in conservative circles—to propose a VAT, which many identify with "socialist Europe." That's OK. Call them anything you want. What is important for readers to remember is that VATs are consumption taxes; and all consumption taxes, including retail sales taxes, are essentially similar to each other in their economic impacts.

More Bold Reforms

Downsizing or Replacing the Corporate Tax

Conventional tax reform is incremental change. Fundamental reform, the topic of the prior chapter, is radical change. This chapter describes six proposals in between conventional and fundamental reform. They add new taxes to the system that replace or significantly downsize the corporate tax. None of these new taxes have been tried in the United States, and except for the VAT, they are untried anywhere else in the world.

The aim of fundamental tax reform proposals is to end income taxation in the United States and replace it with a consumption tax. And in the process, the corporation tax and all its problems are wiped off the map. The proposals in this chapter have less-sweeping goals. Some are bold efforts at integrating corporate and individual income taxes. Some are designed to move the United States more in the direction of a consumption tax while still retaining some aspects of income taxation.

Before describing these intrinsic structural changes, we should do a reality check on the stuff around the edges of these changes—the proposed elimination of all or most tax breaks. In general, all tax reforms aspire to jettison tax expenditures from our tax laws in order to promote fairness, simplicity, and economic growth. Unfortunately, if any of these proposals came close to enactment, it is almost certain the changes would include complicated transition rules and the retention of tax breaks for many special interest groups. The repeal of our current income tax system does not mean politics as we know it will be transformed. Because the issue of eliminating tax breaks is largely separable from the restructuring of a tax system, we should judge proposed changes on the structural changes that define them.

Sweeping Integration Proposals

The Treasury Department under President George H.W. Bush wanted to eliminate the corporate tax biases that favor debt over equity and favor non-corporate over corporate investment. In January 1992, the Treasury released its plan to replace the rickety-old corporate tax with a bold new tax called the *Comprehensive Business Income Tax (CBIT)*. It is called "comprehensive" because returns on all capital—whether paid out as dividends or interest—would be subject to one and the same entity-level tax. It is called a "business" tax because it would apply to all businesses, not just to currently taxable Subchapter C corporations. And it is called an "income" tax because the proposal, while eliminating the double tax on corporate profits, would not move the United States to a consumption tax system.

Under the proposal, as with several other more conventional integration proposals (discussed in Chapter 3), dividends would not be subject to tax at the individual level. The truly innovative feature of the CBIT is the treatment of interest on business debt. It would not be taxed at the individual level. And it would not be deductible at the business level. By doing this, all returns to business investment—both debt and equity—would be treated equally. All would be taxed once, at the business level. (The Treasury at the time suggested a 31.5 percent rate.) And all would be tax-free at the individual level. Furthermore, under the CBIT, capital purchases would be depreciated, not expensed.

The main political problem for the CBIT is that corporations with significant interest expense would be subject to a major tax increase. After President Bush lost the 1992 election, the CBIT faded from view. It was momentarily resurrected in 2002 when the Treasury Department under President George W. Bush explored it as an option. But the administration ended up proposing a less ambitious approach to integration: a dividend exclusion. As it wound through the legislative process, that proposal eventually morphed into the 15 percent preferential rate on dividends that we have today.

Professor Edward Kleinbard of the University of Southern California has proposed a tax that, like the CBIT, would eliminate double taxation of corporate profits and eliminate the differential tax treatment of debt and equity.

Kleinbard, a former chief of staff of the congressional Joint Committee on Taxation, calls his proposal the *Business Enterprise Income Tax (BEIT)*. As under CBIT, all businesses would be subject to tax, and capital purchases would be depreciated. The main difference is that, while under the CBIT businesses get no deductions for interest or for dividends, under the BEIT they would now receive a deduction equal to a risk-free rate of return on invested capital. Kleinbard calls this deduction a *cost of capital allowance (COCA)*. Individual investors holding stocks and bonds would include the COCA in taxable income each year instead of interest and capital gains. What about the investor income in excess of COCA? Business would pay tax on that excess. Individuals would be exempt from tax on that excess.

Both the CBIT and the BEIT are business taxes that eliminate double tax of corporate profits but leave the United States with an income tax. To promote capital formation and economic growth, many believe the United States should substitute consumption taxation for income taxation. It is possible to convert the CBIT into a consumption tax by allowing businesses to expenses, rather depreciate, their capital investments.

In 2005, the president's Advisory Panel on Tax Reform proposed the *Growth and Investment Tax (GIT)*. Like the CBIT, all businesses are subject to the tax and businesses would not be allowed to deduct interest. But unlike the CBIT, capital purchases are expensed. (It turns out that the structure of the GIT is the same as that of business component of the Flat Tax and of the X-tax, discussed in the previous chapter.) Unlike the Flat Tax and X-tax, the GIT system taxes dividends, interest, and capital gains at the individual level. Because this capital income is taxed at a preferential 15 percent rate, the GIT, in addition to eliminating the double tax on corporate profits, moves the United States more in the direction of an overall consumption tax.

It is understandable for the newcomer to be disoriented by the alphabet soup of business tax options. One key thing to remember about the three taxes just described—the CBIT, the BEIT, and the GIT—is that while they may resemble a VAT, they *do* allow deductions for wages and other employee compensation. This is not a minor detail, as wages are often the largest component of a business's deductible expenses.

More VATs

Professor Michael Graetz of Columbia University Law School has proposed a *Competitive Tax Plan* for the United States. The plan calls for the imposition of a European-style VAT with a rate between 10 and 15 percent. The revenue raised from the VAT would be used to eliminate 90 percent of taxpayers from the income tax rolls. Before World War II only the wealthiest Americans paid income tax. The Graetz proposal would convert the U.S. income tax back from a "mass tax" to a "class tax." Graetz, a former Deputy Assistant Secretary of the Treasury, would also use VAT revenue to reduce the top individual and corporate tax rates to 25 percent.

With 100 million fewer taxpayers filing income tax returns, the proposal would greatly reduce the national compliance burden. Replacing income tax revenues with consumption tax revenues would increase investment and economic growth. Despite this, conservatives object to the plan because they fear establishment of a VAT would make future tax increases more likely. And even if it results in higher compliance costs, they feel it is important that most Americans pay at least some nominal amount of income tax.

In December 2007, the Treasury Department floated a proposal that would impose a VAT of between 5 and 6 percent and use the revenue to repeal the corporate tax and individual income tax on business income. Because the name "VAT" has negative connotations for many, the Treasury called its new tax the *Business Activities Tax (BAT)*. Replacing the corporation tax, one of the most economically damaging of taxes, with one of the least distorting taxes would provide a significant boost to economic growth.

Market Capitalization Tax

The objective of the *Market Capitalization Tax* is neither to eliminate the double tax on corporate profits nor to move the United States toward a consumption tax. Proposed by Professor Calvin Johnson of the University of Texas Law School, the tax would replace the loophole-ridden and highly complex corporate tax with a simple, low-rate tax on the market value of the outstanding debt and equity of publicly traded companies. The tax would be imposed quarterly at a rate of 0.2 percent (20 basis points). So, a corporation with market capitalization of $300 billion (like Apple, for example) would pay $2.4 billion annually.

Because the value of both outstanding debt and equity would be subject to tax, the tax would not favor debt over equity. The proposal would eliminate the inequity of large, publicly traded partnerships escaping corporate tax while publicly traded corporations incur large tax bills. The proposal would remove incentives for most conventional types of tax planning. The proposal would be so simple that tax returns would not even have to be filed because the IRS could ascertain market value from public sources and simply send the company a bill!

Summary

Although not as sweeping as a Flat or a Fair Tax, all of the proposals discussed in this chapter would be huge changes in U.S. tax law—larger in impact than even the landmark Tax Reform Act of 1986. The political difficulties would be enormous. Although all are designed to be revenue-neutral, history tells us that the losers scream louder than the winners. Because the size of the changes, there would be considerable uncertainty about direct effects on each taxpayer and the indirect effects on the overall economy. Even if the new taxes are simpler, there will be necessarily increased complexity during the transition period, when all taxpayers and the IRS must deal with the new and the old tax systems simultaneously. All the proposals would also create complications for states whose taxes may or may not continue to conform to federal taxes. In taxation, the gap between chalkboard and reality can be vast.

The Budget and Political Reality

Something Impossible Is Going to Happen

Before the Great Recession of 2007-2009, all proposals for tax reform—whether big or small, fundamental or incremental, untried or traditional, liberal or conservative—shared one common feature. None of them raised revenue (and a few were overall tax cuts). Enacting tax reform is difficult enough. It is often called the "impossible dream." No tax reform advocate wants to take on the additional political baggage of simultaneously raising taxes in a nation as anti-tax as the United States. But tax reformers no longer have that luxury. Tax reformers can no more ignore the effect of the burgeoning federal debt than the tides can ignore the gravitational pull of the moon. Even if you share the views of the current Republican leadership in Congress that tax reform should not raise revenue, there is no denying that that the national debt casts a long shadow over any tax debate.

The United States has two types of deficit problems. Except for a brief respite at the end of the Clinton administration, politics-as-usual has left the U.S. government spending far more than it collects in revenue. The results are those annual budget deficits that lie in plain sight. Meanwhile, less visible to the public, as time marched forward and Americans on average grew older, the United States kept moving closer to the inevitable financial collapse of Social Security and Medicare. Until recently, with the federal debt hovering around 40 percent of GDP, well within the bounds of historical and international precedent for sound government finance, everybody assumed it would be many election cycles before definitive action would be needed.

The 2007–2009 recession and turmoil in financial markets changed all that. There was an automatic increase in government spending on social programs and a rapid decline in the tax revenue that depends so heavily on the strength of employment and the stock market. In addition, Congress enacted spending cuts and tax decreases to stimulate aggregate demand. This catapulted our federal debt from 40 to 69 percent of GDP in less than four years.

The 2011 Deficit Reduction Deal

On August 1, 2011, by a vote of 269 to 161 (Republicans: 174 to 66; Democrats: 95 to 95), the House of Representative approved the Budget Control Act of 2011. On August 2, by a vote of 74 to 26 (Democrats: 45 to 6; Republicans: 28 to 19; Independents: 1 to 1), the Senate followed suit. President Obama signed the bill into law the same day. Any relief this new law provided from concerns about deteriorating federal finances was short-lived. On August 5, the Standard & Poor's bond-rating agency downgraded U.S. government debt from AAA to AA+ and sent financial markets into turmoil.

The landmark budget legislation was the result of months of heated negotiations in which Republicans threatened not to raise the government's debt ceiling if significant spending cuts were not enacted. In the end, Congress and President agreed to a deficit reduction plan that the CBO estimated will reduce the deficit by $2.1 trillion over ten years.

That's a lot of money. And for Congress to agree to spending cuts of any significant magnitude is certainly a political milestone. But what is its economic significance? Is it enough deficit reduction to stabilize the federal government's finances?

To answer that question you need make projections of future deficits. This cannot all be all scientific because it requires making educated guesses about future political outcomes. The best anybody can do is pick clear, middle-of-the-road assumptions and be transparent about the choices.

Figure 15-1 shows projections of future deficits before and after passage of the Budget Control Act of 2011 (BCA11). The pre-BCA11 line makes the following assumptions: that discretionary spending grows with inflation (and therefore shrinks as a percentage of GDP); that Medicare, Medicaid, and Social Security proceed as under current law with the exception that limits on physician Medicare reimbursement are not allowed to take effect; that troop levels in Iraq and Afghanistan are reduced to 45,000 by 2015; that the individual alternative minimum tax is indexed for inflation (and not allowed to expand its reach to tens of millions of middle-class taxpayers); that the package of repeatedly expiring tax provisions are extended indefinitely; and, most importantly, that the Bush tax cuts originally set to expire at the end of 2010, and now scheduled to expire at the end of 2012, are all extended indefinitely. These assumptions are largely consistent with those made by the CBO, by the White House, and by other budget experts in their projections of deficits under "current policy."

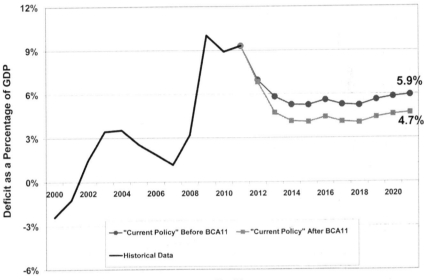

Figure 15-1. Historical and projected deficits, 2000–2021. Source: Congressional Budget Office and others (see Appendix A).

The pre-BCA11 line shows that after the effects of the recession pass, projected deficits are expected to decline. But in the second half of the next decade, the effect of long-term budget problems overwhelms federal finances and the deficit grows steadily through 2021 and beyond. Under this current policy projection, the federal deficit equals 5.9 percent of GDP in 2021.

The deficit reduction in the new legislation works in two stages. Stage one reduces spending by approximately $900 billion. These cuts are specific and explicitly included in the legislation. Stage two calls for additional cuts in spending of $1.2 trillion—divided evenly between defense and Medicare—

that will come into effect in 2013 if by December 23, 2011 Congress does not approve a deficit reduction plan devised by a special bipartisan, bi-cameral 12-member joint select committee.

The post-BCA11 line in Figure 15-1 shows projected deficits, including both phases of deficit reduction in the new legislation. Under this projection, the federal deficit equals 4.7 percent of GDP in 2021. In other words, the new law is projected to result in a decrease in the deficit of 1.2 percent of GDP for that year.

Sustainability and Balance

When it comes to determining how large the deficit should be, there are two standards that are most commonly discussed. The first has a lot of in-tuitive appeal: *balancing the budget*. The second is a concept used by econo-mists: *sustainability*.

Currently, there is a growing interest—particularly among Republicans—about enacting an amendment to the Constitution to require a balanced federal budget. The most common objection to a balanced-budget amend-ment is that it would eliminate the ability of federal government to fight re-cessions with deficit-increasing stimulus. Another issue usually glossed over by proponents of a balanced-budget amendment is that the magnitude of deficit reduction required to balance the budget is so enormous that it is hard to conceive how that the political system as we know it could ever agree to the necessary policies.

As shown in Figure 15-1, the projected deficit in 2021 is 4.7 percent of GDP. It was extremely difficult for Congress and the president to agree to the August 2011 legislation that reduced the projected deficit in 2021 by ap-proximately 1.2 percent of GDP. Balancing the federal budget would require more than four times that amount of additional deficit reduction in 2021.

An alternative goal is budget *sustainability*. When economists say they want to put federal finances on a sustainable path, they mean they want the fed-eral debt to grow no faster than GDP. In other words, the level of out-standing debt relative to GDP does not increase.

In terms of annual deficits, sustainability requires the federal deficit be re-duced to about 3 percent of GDP. Even though this is a far more modest goal than balancing the budget, achieving sustainable federal finance would still be an onerous political task. To get the deficit-to-GDP level down to 3 percent from its currently projected 4.7 percent level in 2021 would require deficit reduction of another 1.7 percent of GDP in 2021 on top of the 1.2 percent of GDP agreed to in August. Currently, 1.2 percent of GDP is about $180 billion.

The proverbial 600-pound gorilla in this room is the fate of the Bush tax cuts scheduled to expire at the end of 2012. Allowing them to expire for all income classes would reduce the deficit in 2021 by about 3.1 percent of GDP—more than enough to put federal finances on a sustainable path. But Republicans are adamantly opposed to curtailing any of these cuts. And President Obama wants the cuts to be extended for families with incomes below $250,000. The Obama proposal of allowing the Bush cuts to lapse only for households with incomes over $250,000 would reduce the deficit by approximately 1 percent of GDP.

Prospects for Corporate Tax Reform

What are the chances corporate tax reform will actually happen? In the Beltway prediction game, it is always safe to be pessimistic and cynical. By design our federal government is slow to adopt change. Reform is antithetical to special interests, and special interests have both the motivation and influence to dominate the politics of issues that the public does not have the attention span to follow. These factors have always been obstacles to reform.

Our large, unprecedented debt overhang makes reform even more difficult. There are three reasons. First, there is little or no hope that Congress will simultaneously cut taxes when it reforms the corporate tax. A tax cut would certainly lubricate the process. Second, the closing of many revenue-raising corporate loopholes may take place before reform is on the table. For example, there is some talk of closing loopholes in order to reduce the deficit. The most politically vulnerable loopholes will be attacked first. If they are used for deficit reduction, that takes away the most combustible revenue-raising fuel for building the tax reform fire.

Finally, there are the physical and time constraints of the legislative process. All previous tax reforms have been time-consuming and complicated. In the House of Representatives, revenue measures are the jurisdiction of the Ways and Means Committee. Its counterpart in the Senate is the Committee on Finance. These committees also have jurisdiction over Medicare, Medicaid, Social Security, and management of the public debt. No matter how great the clamor for corporate tax reform, it must be scheduled in between or after other sweeping changes in America's fiscal framework.

Even after passage of the Budget Control Act of 2011, the U.S. government is in deep financial trouble. If we remain on automatic pilot we will go over the fiscal abyss unless spending cuts and tax increases previously considered unthinkable are enacted. Something impossible—like a major cut to Social Security, or a large tax increase, or a default on government debt—is going to happen. Hopefully, corporate tax reform that broadens the base, lowers the rate, simplifies, and promote economic growth will be included in the major fiscal realignment the government so desperately needs.

Throughout this book, I have tried to be realistic in my assessment of the political difficulties in passing corporate tax reform and not overstate the economics benefits. You, the reader, deserve that. That does not mean that corporate tax reform doesn't deserve to be a priority for our leaders in Washington.

Summary

Corporate tax reform is thick in the air in Washington, D.C. But it is a long way from making news to making law. Corporate tax reform will not be glamorous work. Politicians will have to gain an in-depth understanding of our corporate tax system and how it affects the economy. They will have to be thinking thoughts that cannot be expressed in sound bites. They will have to roll up their sleeves more and talk into microphones less. They will have to stand up to well-paid, well-connected lobbyists who are working full-time to change their minds. But corporate tax reform is something real that they can do to make our economy more competitive and create jobs. And if that means lawmakers have to work long hours, we'll be glad to bring the coffee.

Notes on Tables and Figures

Figure 2-1. Profits as a percentage of GDP, 1955–2010. U.S. Department of Commerce, Bureau of Economic Analysis, National Income and Product Accounts Table 1.12, "National Income by Type of Income" and Table 1.1.5, "Gross Domestic Product."

Figure 2-2. Shares of national income, 1999–2010 average. U.S. Department of Commerce, Bureau of Economic Analysis, National Income and Product Accounts Table 1.12. "National Income by Type of Income."

Figure 2-3. Corporate tax revenue, 1999–2010. President's Budget for Fiscal Year 2012, Historical Tables. Table 2.1, "Receipts by Source: 1934–2016," http://www.whitehouse.gov/omb/budget/Historicals.

Figure 2-4. The composition of federal revenue, 1999–2010 average. President's Budget for Fiscal Year 2012, Historical Tables. Table 2.1, "Receipts by Source: 1934–2016," http://www.whitehouse.gov/omb/budget/Historicals.

Figure 2-5. Corporate tax receipts as a percentage of GDP, 1955–2010. President's Budget for Fiscal Year 2012, Table 2.3, "Receipts by Source as Percentages of GDP: 1934–2016," http://www.whitehouse.gov/omb/budget/Historicals.

Figure 2-6. U.S. federal corporate tax rate, 1955–2011. Tax Foundation, "Federal Corporate Income Tax Rates, Income Years 1909–2008," August 17, 2008, http://www.taxfoundation.org/taxdata/show/ 2140.html.

Figure 2-7. Corporate tax revenue, 2008, by size of corporation. Internal Revenue Service, Statistics of Income Division, SOI Tax Stats, Table 5, "Returns of Active Corporations, Selected Balance Sheet, Income Statement, and Tax Items. Classified by: Sector, Size of Business Receipts," http://www.irs.gov/taxstats/article/0,,id=170691,00.html.

Table 2-1. The Declining Effective Tax Rates of America's Most Profitable Corporations. Annual 10-K reports of individual companies filed with the Securities and Exchange Commission, on the Internet at each company's web site under the tab labeled "investor relations."

Table 3-1. Tax Bias Against Dividends: Combined Individual and Corporate Tax Rates on Corporate Profits. Author's calculations. Assumptions: Before-tax rate of return = 10%; corporate tax rate = 35%; dividend and capital gains tax rates = 15%.

Figure 5-1. U.S and OECD average corporate tax rates, 1981–2011. Organisation for Economic Co-operation and Development, Revenue Statistics, Table II.1 "Basic (non-targeted) corporate income tax rates," http://www.oecd.org/ctp/taxdatabase.

Table 5-1. Corporate Tax Rates (National and Local) in 2011. Organisation for Economic Co-operation and Development, Revenue Statistics, Table II.1 "Basic (non-targeted) corporate income tax rates," http://www.oecd.org/ctp/taxdatabase.

Table 6-1. An Example of the Value of Accelerated Depreciation. Author's calculations. Assumptions: Tax rate of 35 percent and discount rate of 8 percent.

Table 7-1. The Graduated Corporate Rate Structure. Section 11(b) of the Internal Revenue Code.

Table 7-2. The Corporate Tax Expenditure Budget. *President's Budget for Fiscal Year 2012, Analytical Perspectives,* Chapter 17, "Tax Expenditures," http://www.whitehouse.gov/sites/default/files/omb/budget/fy2012/assets/receipts.pdf.

Table 8-1. Foreign (non-U.S.) Share of Worldwide Profits of Some Leading U.S. Multinationals. Annual 10-K reports of individual companies filed with the Securities and Exchange Commission, on the Internet at each company's web site under the tab labeled "investor relations."

Figure 9-1. U.S. multinational job creation, 1999–2008. U.S. Department of Commerce, Bureau of Economic Analysis, U.S. Direct Investment Abroad: Operations of U.S. Parent Companies and Their Foreign Affiliates, Comprehensive Financial and Operating Data, Table III.H1, "Employment and Compensation of Employees of Affiliates, Country by Type," and Table 3, "Selected Data for All U.S. Parents, by Industry of U.S. Parent," http://www.bea.gov/scb/account-articles/international/ iidguide.htm#link12b.

Figure 9-2. Growth of foreign affiliates of U.S. multinationals, 1999–2007. U.S. Department of Commerce, Bureau of Economic Analysis, U.S. Direct Investment Abroad: Operations of U.S. Parent Companies and Their Foreign Affiliates, Comprehensive Financial and Operating Data, Table III.E, "Income Statement of Affiliates, Country by Account," and Table III.B1–2, "Balance Sheet of Affiliates, Country by Account," http://www.bea.gov/scb/account-articles/international/iidguide.htm#link12b,

Table 9-1. High Rates of Profit in Low-Tax Jurisdictions. U.S. Department of Commerce, Bureau of Economic Analysis, U.S. Direct Investment Abroad: Operations of U.S. Parent Companies and Their Foreign Affiliates, Comprehensive Financial and Operating Data, Table III.E, "Income Statement of Affiliates, Country by Account," and Table III.B1–2, "Balance Sheet of Affiliates, Country by Account," http://www.bea.gov/scb/account-articles/international/iidguide.htm#link12b.

Figure 10-1. The fantastic growth of S corporations, 1980–2008 (in millions). Internal Revenue Service, Statistics of Income Division, SOI Tax Stats, S Corporation Statistics, Table 1, "S Corporations: Total Receipts and Deductions, Portfolio Income, Rental Income, and Total Net Income, by Major Industry," http://www.irs.gov/taxstats/article/0,,id=171033,00.html; and SOI Integrated Business Data, Table 1, "Selected financial data on businesses,1980–2007," http://www.irs.gov/taxstats/bustaxstats/article/0,, id=152029,00.html.

Figure 10-2. The rapid rise of LLPs. Internal Revenue Service, Statistics of Income Division, SOI Partnership Tax Stats, Partnership Statistics by Sector and Industry, "General Partnerships, Limited Partnerships, and Limited Liability Companies," http://www.irs.gov/taxstats/bustaxstats/article/ 0,,id= 97127,00.html; and SOI Integrated Business Data, Table 1, "Selected financial data on businesses,1980–2007," http://www.irs.gov/taxstats/ bustaxstats/ article/0,,id=152029,00.html.

Figure 10-3. Sole proprietorships, 1980–2009. Internal Revenue Service, Statistics of Income Division, SOI Tax Stats, Non-Farm Sole Proprietorship Statistics, "Business Receipts, Selected Deductions, Payroll, and Net Income," http://www.irs.gov/taxstats/indtaxstats/article/ 0,,id=134481,00.html;

and SOI Integrated Business Data, Table 1, "Selected financial data on businesses,1980–2007," http://www.irs.gov/taxstats/bustaxstats/article/0,,id=152029,00.html.

Figure 10-4. Average receipts of sole proprietorships, 1980–2009. Internal Revenue Service, Statistics of Income Division, SOI Tax Stats, Non-Farm Sole Proprietorship Statistics, "Business Receipts, Selected Deductions, Payroll, and Net Income," http://www.irs.gov/taxstats/indtaxstats/article/0,,id=134481,00.html; and SOI Integrated Business Data, Table 1, "Selected financial data on businesses,1980–2007," http://www.irs.gov/taxstats/bustaxstats/article/0,,id=152029,00.html.

Table 10-1. Business Shares by Filing Status, 1980–2008. Internal Revenue Service, Statistics of Income Division, Integrated Business Data, Table 1, http://www.irs.gov/taxstats/bustaxstats/article/0,,id=152029,00.html; C corporation data, Table 12, "Returns of Active Corporations, Other Than Forms 1120S, 1120-REIT, and 1120-RIC," http://www.irs.gov/taxstats/bustaxstats/article/0,,id=112834,00.html; S corporation, Table 7, "Returns of Active Corporations, Form 1120S," http://www.irs.gov/taxstats/bustaxstats/article/0,,id=112834,00.html; Partnerships, "All Partnerships, Total Assets, Trade or Business Income and Deductions, Portfolio Income, Rental Income, and Total Net Income," http://www.irs.gov/taxstats/bustaxstats/article/0,,id=130919,00.html; and Non-farm sole proprietorships, "Business Receipts, Selected Deductions, Payroll, and Net Income," http://www.irs.gov/taxstats/indtaxstats/article/0,,id=134481,00.html.

Table 10-2. Subchapter S Corporations with $50 Million or More in Receipts, 2008. Internal Revenue Service, Statistics of Income Division, SOI Tax Stats, Table 4, "Returns of Active Corporations, Form 1120S, Total receipts and deductions, portfolio income, rental income and total net income. Classified by: Size of business receipts and sector," http://www.irs.gov/taxstats/article/0,,id=171053,00.html.

Table 10-3. Partnerships with $100 Million or More in Assets, 2008. Internal Revenue Service, Statistics of Income Division, SOI Tax Stats, Partnership Data by Size of Total Assets, "All Partnerships, Total Assets, Trade or Business Income and Deductions, Portfolio Income, Rental Income, and Total Net Income," http://www.irs.gov/taxstats/bustaxstats/article/0,,id=130919,00.html.

Figure 11-1. State corporation taxes as a share of U.S. domestic profits, 1948–2009. U.S. Census Bureau, state government tax collections, historical data; spreadsheet available at http://www.census.gov/govs/qtax/publications.php; and U.S. Department of Commerce, Bureau of Economic

Analysis, National Income and Product Accounts Table 1.12, "National Income by Type of Income."

Table 11-1. State Corporation Taxes, Rates, and Revenue. Tax Foundation, "State Corporate Income Tax Rates, 2000–2011," March 11, 2011, http://www.taxfoundation.org/taxdata/show/230.html; and U.S. Census Bureau, state government tax collections, historical data; spreadsheet available at http://www.census.gov/govs/qtax/publications.php.

Table 12-1. Corporate AMT Revenues, 1987–2008 (in Billions). Internal Revenue Service, Statistics of Income Division, SOI Tax Stats, Corporation Source Book of Statistics of Income, "Returns of Active Corporations, Balance Sheet, Income Statement, and Selected Items, by Minor Industry, by Size of Total Assets"; and Andrew B. Lyon, "Corporate Alternative Minimum Tax," in Joseph J. Cordes, Robert D. Ebel, and Jane Gravelle, eds., *Encyclopedia of Taxation and Tax Policy*, Washington D.C., Urban Institute, 2005.

Table 13-1. VATs around the World. Organisation for Economic Cooperation and Development, Revenue Statistics, Table IV.1 "Rates of value added tax (general sales tax)," http://www.oecd.org/ctp/taxdatabase.

Table 13-2. The Equivalence of the Flat Tax and the VAT. Author's calculations.

Figure 15-1. Historical and projected deficits, 2000–2021. Projections for this figure combine data from three sources: [A] CBO, *Budget and Economic Outlook: Fiscal Years 2011 to 2021*, http://www.cbo.gov/ftpdocs/120xx/doc12039/01-26_FY2011Outlook.pdf, Jan. 2011; [B] CBO, *An Analysis of the President's Budgetary Proposals for Fiscal Year 2012*, http://www.cbo.gov/ftpdocs/121xx/doc12130/04-15-AnalysisPresidentsBudget.pdf, April 2011; and [C] CBO, "CBO Analysis of August 1 Budget Control Act," Letter to the Honorable John Boehner and the Honorable Harry Reid, http://www.cbo.gov/ftpdocs/123xx/doc12357/ BudgetControlActAug1.pdf, August 1, 2011.

The pre-BCA11 baseline is computed by combining the current law baseline from Table 1.1 of [B] with "Incorporate final 2011 appropriations" from Table 1 of [C] and the following four items from Table 1-7 of [A]: "Reduce the Number of Troops Deployed for Certain Types of Overseas Military Operations to 45,000 by 2015"; "Maintain Medicare's Payment Rates for Physicians at the 2011 Level"; "Extend Certain Income Tax and Estate and Gift Tax Provisions Scheduled to Expire on December 31, 2012, and Index the AMT for Inflation"; and "Extend Other Expiring Tax Provisions." The post-BCA11 baseline equals the pre-PCA11 baseline plus "Total Effect on the Deficit Excluding Provisions Related to the Joint Select

Committee on Deficit Reduction" and "Provisions Related to the Joint Select Committee on Deficit Reduction" from Table 3 of [C]. GDP projections used to compute deficits as a percentage of GDP are from Table 1.2 of [B].

Further Reading

General Background

Congressional Budget Office. "Taxing Capital Income: Effective Rates and Approaches to Reform." October 2005.

Gravelle, Jane G. and Thomas L. Hungerford. "Corporate Tax Reform: Issues for Congress." Congressional Research Service, April 2008.

Gravelle, Jane G. *The Economic Effects of Taxing Capital Income*. Cambridge, MA: MIT Press, 1994.

Shaviro, Daniel N. *Decoding the U.S. Corporate Tax*. Washington, DC: Urban Institute, 2009.

Sheppard, Lee A. "What Do Corporate Tax Managers Want?" *Tax Notes*, March 7, 2011.

Sullivan, Martin A. "A Hitchhiker's Guide to Corporate Tax Reform." *Tax Notes*, December 7, 2009.

Sullivan, Martin A. "Corporate Reform: Time to Think Outside the Box." *Tax Notes*, March 28, 2011.

Sullivan, Martin A. "Corporate Tax Reform—or Else?" *Tax Notes*, June 22, 2009.

Sullivan, Martin A. "Reported Corporate Effective Tax Rates Down Since Late 1990s." *Tax Notes*, February 25, 2008.

Sullivan, Martin A. "Tax Incentives and Economists." *Tax Notes*, April 3, 2006.

Sullivan, Martin A. "Tax Reform Fantasy." *Tax Notes*, November 22, 2010.

Sullivan, Martin A. "The Fate of Tax Reform Depends on the Tea Party." *Tax Notes*, January 2011.

Sullivan, Martin A. "A New Era in Corporate Taxation." Testimony before the Senate Committee on Finance, June 13, 2006.

Tax Reform in the 1980s

Birnbaum, Jeffrey H. and Alan S. Murray. Showdown at Gucci Gulch: Lawmakers, Lobbyists, and the Unlikely Triumph of Tax Reform. New York, NY: Vintage, 1987.

Brownlee, W. Elliot. Federal Taxation in America: A Short History. Washington, DC: Woodrow Wilson Center Press, 2004.

Kocieniewski, David. "G.E.'s Strategies Let It Avoid Taxes Altogether." *New York Times*, March 24, 2011.

Office of the President. The President's Tax Proposals to the Congress for Fairness, Growth, and Simplicity. 1985.

Office of the Secretary, Treasury Department. Tax Reform for Fairness, Simplicity, and Economic Growth: The Treasury Department Report to the President. 1984.

Regan, Donald T. *For the Record: From Wall Street to Washington*. New York, NY: Harcourt Brace Jovanovich, 1988.

Steuerle, C. Eugene. *Contemporary U.S. Tax Policy, Second Edition*. Washington, DC: Urban Institute Press, 2008.

Proposed Incremental Reforms

President's Advisory Panel on Federal Tax Reform. "Simple, Fair, and Pro-Growth: Proposals to Fix America's Tax System." November 2005, *available at* http://www.taxreformpanel.gov/final-report.

President's Council of Economic Advisers. Economic Report of the President 2007, Chapter 3, "Pro-Growth Tax Policy."

Sullivan, Martin A. "Winners and Losers in Corporate Tax Reform." *Tax Notes*, February 14, 2011.

Yin, Gerge K. "Corporate Tax Reform, Finally, After 100 Years," in *Toward Tax Reform: Recommendations for President Obama's Task Force.* Tax Analysts, *available at* http://www.tax.org.

Zodrow, George R. and Charles E. McLure, Jr. "Time for US Tax Reform? The Tax Reform Panel's Recommendations." *Bulletin of the International Bureau for Fiscal Documentation,* April 2006.

Zolt, Eric M. "Reform the Taxation of Business Income," in *Toward Tax Reform: Recommendations for President Obama's Task Force.* Falls Church, VA: Tax Analysts, 2010, *available at* http://www.tax.org.

Fundamental Reforms, Bold Reforms

Buckley, John and Diane Lim Rogers. "Is a National Retail Sales Tax in Our Future?" *Tax Notes,* September 13, 2004, p. 1277.

Bradford, David. *Untangling the Income Tax.* Cambridge, MA: Harvard University Press, 1986.

Burton, David R. and Dan R. Mastromarco. "The National Sales Tax: Moving Beyond the Idea." *Tax Notes,* May 27, 1996, p. 1237.

Edwards, Chris. "Replacing the Scandal-Plagued Corporate Income Tax with a Cash-Flow Tax." Cato Institute, August 2003, *available at* http://www.cato.org/pubs/pas/pa484.pdf.

Gale, William G. and Benjamin H. Harris. "A Value-Added Tax for the United States: Part of the Solution." Brookings Institution and Tax Policy Center, July 2010, http://www.brookings.edu/~/media/Files/rc/papers/2010/0721_vat_for_us_gale/0721_vat_for_us_gale.pdf.

Graetz, Michael J. *100 Million Unnecessary Returns: A Simple, Fair, and Competitive Tax Plan for the United States.* New Haven, CT: Yale University Press, 2008.

Johnson, Calvin H. "Replace the Corporate Tax with a Market Capitalization Tax." *Tax Notes,* December 10, 2007.

Keen, Michael, Mahmood Pradhan, Kenneth Kang, and Ruud de Mooij. "Raising the Consumption Tax in Japan: Why, When, How?" IMF Staff Discussion Note, June 2011.

Kleinbard, Edward D. "The Business Enterprise Income Tax: A Prospectus." *Tax Notes,* January 3, 2005.

Rabushka, Alvin and Robert E. Hall, *The Flat Tax*. Stanford, CA: Hoover Institution Press, 1985.

Rosenberg, Joseph and Eric Toder. "Effects of Imposing a Value-added Tax to Replace Payroll Taxes or Corporate Taxes." *Tax Notes*, April 8, 2010.

Sullivan, Martin A. "Getting to a VAT." *Tax Notes*, April 19, 2010.

Sullivan, Martin A. "VAT Increase for Japan No Longer Taboo." *Tax Notes*, July 12, 2010.

Sullivan, Martin A. "VAT Lessons From Canada." *Tax Notes*, May 3, 2010.

Tax Analysts. The VAT Reader: What a Federal Consumption Tax Would Mean for America. April 5, 2010.

U.S. Department of the Treasury. "Approaches to Improve the Competitiveness of the U.S. Business Tax System for the 21st Century." December 20, 2007, *available at* http://www.ustreas.gov/press/releases/reports/hp749_approachesstudy.pdf.

U.S. Department of the Treasury. "Approaches to Improve the Competitiveness of the U.S. Business Tax System for the 21st Century." December 20, 2007.

U.S. Department of the Treasury. "Report of the Department of the Treasury on Integration of the Individual and Corporate Tax Systems." January 1992, *available at* http://www.ustreas.gov/offices/tax-policy/library/integration-paper.

U.S. Department of the Treasury. "Treasury Conference on Business Taxation and Global Competitiveness Background Paper." July 23, 2007, *available at* http://www.treasury.gov/press-center/press-releases/Documents/07230%20r.pdf.

Viard, Alan D., Robert Carroll, and Scott Ganz. "The X Tax: The Progressive Consumption Tax America Needs?" American Enterprise Institute, December 2008, http://www.aei.org/outlook/29082.

Corporate Tax Basics and Integration

Altshuler, Rosanne, Benjamin H. Harris, and Eric Toder. "Capital Income Taxation and Progressivity in a Global Economy," Tax Policy Center, April 26, 2011, http://www.taxpolicycenter.org/UploadedPDF/412328-Capital-Income-Taxation.pdf.

Auerbach, Alan J. "The Choice Between Income and Consumption Taxes: A Primer." NBER Working Paper 12307, 2006.

Auerbach, Alan J. "Who Bears the Corporate Tax? A Review of What We Know." NBER Working Paper 11686, 2005.

Bankman, Joseph and David Weisbach. "The Superiority of an Ideal Consumption Tax over an Ideal Income Tax." *Stanford Law Review*, March 2006.

Chirinko, Robert S., Steven M. Fazzari, and Andrew P. Meyer. "How Responsive is Business Capital Formation to its User Cost? An Exploration with Micro Data." *Journal of Public Economics*, 1999.

Congressional Budget Office. *Corporate Income Tax Rates: International Comparisons.* November 2005.

Gentry, William M. "A Review of the Evidence on the Incidence of the Corporate Income Tax." Department of the Treasury, Office of Tax Analysis, 2007.

Graetz, Michael J. and Alvin C. Warren, *Integration of the U.S. Corporate and Individual Income Taxes: The Treasury Department and American Law Institute Reports.* Falls Church, VA.: Tax Analysts, 1998.

Gravelle, Jane G. and Kent Smetters. "Who Bears the Burden of the Corporate Tax in the Open Economy?" NBER Working Paper 8280, 2001.

Halperin, Daniel. "Mitigating the Potential Inequity of Reducing Corporate Rates." *Tax Notes*, February 1, 2010.

Hubbard, Glenn. "Corporate Tax Integration: A View from the Treasury Department." *Journal of Economic Perspectives*, winter 1993.

Jensen, Matthew H. and Aparna Mathur. "Corporate Tax Burden on Labor: Theory and Empirical Evidence." *Tax Notes*, June 6, 2011, p. 1083.

Joint Committee on Taxation. Present Law and Background Relating to Tax Treatment of Business Debt. JCX-41-11, July 11, 2011.

Marr, Chuck and Brian Highsmith. "Six Tests for Corporate Tax Reform." Center for Budget and Policy Priorities, February 28, 2011, http://www.cbpp.org/files/2-28-11tax.pdf.

Olson, Pamela F. "Tax Reform and the Tax Treatment of Debt and Equity." Statement to the Committee on Ways & Means United States, House of Representatives, and the Committee On Finance, United States Senate, July 13, 2011.

Sheppard, Lee A. "Do Corporate Tax Rates Matter? *Tax Notes*, March 7, 2011.

Bank, Steven A. "The Rise and Fall of Post-World War II Corporate Tax Reform," *Law & Contemporary Problems*, 2010.

Sullivan, Martin A. "Deleveraging the Tax Code." *Tax Notes*, September 29, 2008.

Sullivan, Martin A. "Why Reported Effective Corporate Tax Rates Are Falling." *Tax Notes*, March 3, 2008.

Toder, Eric and Kim Rueben "Should We Eliminate Taxation of Capital Income?" in Henry J. Aaron, Leonard E. Burman, and C. Eugene Steuerle, eds., *Taxing Capital Income*. Washington, D.C.: Urban Institute Press, 2007.

Tax Rates and Tax Expenditures

Atkinson, Robert D. "Expanding the R&D Tax Credit to Drive Innovation, Competitiveness and Prosperity." Information Technology and Innovation Foundation (http://www.irtif.org), April 2007.

John Buckley. "Tax Expenditure Reform: Some Common Misconceptions." *Tax Notes*, July 18, 2011.

Congressional Budget Office. *Reducing the Deficit: Spending and Revenue Options*. March 10, 2011.

Hodge, Scott A. "Putting Corporate Tax 'Loopholes' in Perspective." Tax Foundation Special Report No. 184, August 3, 2010, http://www.taxfoundation.org/files/sr184.pdf.

Hodge, Scott A. "Ten Benefits of Cutting the U.S. Corporate Tax Rate." Tax Foundation Special Report No. 192, May 11, 2011, http://taxfoundation.org/files/sr192.pdf.

Joint Committee on Taxation. Background Information on Tax Expenditure Analysis and Historical Survey of Tax Joint Committee on Taxation Expenditure Estimates. JCX-15-11, February 28, 2011.

Joint Committee on Taxation. Description of Present Law and Select Proposals Relating to the Oil and Gas Industry. JCX-27-11, May 11, 2011.

Joint Committee on Taxation. Description of Revenue Provisions Contained in the President's Fiscal Year 2010 Budget Proposal Part Two: Business Tax Provisions. JCS-3-09, September 09, 2009.

Joint Committee on Taxation. Oil and Gas Tax Provisions: A Consideration of the President's Fiscal Year 2010 Budget Proposal. JCX-34-09, September 09, 2009.

Joint Committee on Taxation. Present Law and Background Relating to Selected Business Income Tax Provisions. JCX-34-11, June 1, 2011.

Kwall, Jeffrey L. "The Repeal of Graduated Corporate Tax Rates," *Tax Notes*, June 2011.

Merrill, Peter R. "Competitive Tax Rates for U.S. Companies: How Low to Go?" *Tax Notes*, February 23, 2009.

Neubig, Tom. "Expensed Intangibles Have a Zero Effective Tax Rate . . . NOT!" *Tax Notes*, September 10, 2007, p. 959.

Neubig, Tom. "Where's the Applause? Why Most Corporations Prefer a Lower Rate." *Tax Notes*, April 24, 2006.

Shimodoi, Kyodo and Toru Fujioka. "Japan Considers Scrapping Planned Corporate Tax Reduction." Bloomberg, March 29, 2011, http://www.businessweek.com/news/2011-03-29/japan-considers-scrapping-planned-corporate-tax-reduction.html.

Sullivan, Martin A. "Ascending U.K. Conservatives Press Tax Relief—in Moderation." *Tax Notes*, April 10, 2010.

Sullivan, Martin A. "Beyond the Conventional Wisdom: Rate Cuts Beat Expensing." *Tax Notes*, January 28, 2008.

Sullivan, Martin A. "Germany Leads on Jobs, Deficit, and Corporate Tax Policy." *Tax Notes*, November 9, 2009.

Sullivan, Martin A. "High-Tech Companies' Tax Rates Falling." *Tax Notes*, September 4, 2006.

Sullivan, Martin A. "It Is Time to Make All Tax Extenders Permanent." *Tax Notes*, January 11, 2010.

Sullivan, Martin A. "Japan Cuts Corporate Rate, Puts Austerity on Hold." *Tax Notes*, January 3, 2011.

Sullivan, Martin A. "On Corporate Tax Reform, Europe Surpasses the U.S." *Tax Notes*, May 29, 2006.

Sullivan, Martin A. "Tax Credits Ease Economy's Shift to Coal." *Tax Notes*, September 10, 2006.

Sheppard, Lee A. "Do Corporate Tax Rates Matter? *Tax Notes*, March 7, 2011.

Bank, Steven A. "The Rise and Fall of Post-World War II Corporate Tax Reform," *Law & Contemporary Problems*, 2010.

Sullivan, Martin A. "Deleveraging the Tax Code." *Tax Notes*, September 29, 2008.

Sullivan, Martin A. "Why Reported Effective Corporate Tax Rates Are Falling." *Tax Notes*, March 3, 2008.

Toder, Eric and Kim Rueben "Should We Eliminate Taxation of Capital Income?" in Henry J. Aaron, Leonard E. Burman, and C. Eugene Steuerle, eds., *Taxing Capital Income*. Washington, D.C.: Urban Institute Press, 2007.

Tax Rates and Tax Expenditures

Atkinson, Robert D. "Expanding the R&D Tax Credit to Drive Innovation, Competitiveness and Prosperity." Information Technology and Innovation Foundation (http://www.irtif.org), April 2007.

John Buckley. "Tax Expenditure Reform: Some Common Misconceptions." *Tax Notes*, July 18, 2011.

Congressional Budget Office. *Reducing the Deficit: Spending and Revenue Options*. March 10, 2011.

Hodge, Scott A. "Putting Corporate Tax 'Loopholes' in Perspective." Tax Foundation Special Report No. 184, August 3, 2010, http://www.taxfoundation.org/files/sr184.pdf.

Hodge, Scott A. "Ten Benefits of Cutting the U.S. Corporate Tax Rate." Tax Foundation Special Report No. 192, May 11, 2011, http://taxfoundation.org/files/sr192.pdf.

Joint Committee on Taxation. Background Information on Tax Expenditure Analysis and Historical Survey of Tax Joint Committee on Taxation Expenditure Estimates. JCX-15-11, February 28, 2011.

Joint Committee on Taxation. Description of Present Law and Select Proposals Relating to the Oil and Gas Industry. JCX-27-11, May 11, 2011.

Joint Committee on Taxation. Description of Revenue Provisions Contained in the President's Fiscal Year 2010 Budget Proposal Part Two: Business Tax Provisions. JCS-3-09, September 09, 2009.

Sheppard, Lee A. "Ending Deferral Without Repatriating Losses," *Tax Notes*, December 10, 2007.

Sheppard, Lee A. "Defending Obama's International Tax Proposals." *Tax Notes*, June 23, 2009.

Sheppard, Lee A. "Stress Testing Transfer Pricing." *Tax Notes*, March 10, 2009.

Sheppard, Lee A. and Martin A. Sullivan, "Repatriation Aid for the Financial Crisis?" *Tax Notes*, January 5, 2008.

Sheppard, Lee A. and Martin A. Sullivan. "Multinationals Accumulate to Repatriate," *Tax Notes*, January 19, 2009.

Sullivan, Martin A. "A Challenge to Conventional International Tax Wisdom." *Tax Notes*, December 10, 2006.

Sullivan, Martin A. "A Middle Path Between the Arm's-Length and Formulary Methods." *Tax Notes*, January 18, 2010.

Sullivan, Martin A. "A Simple Overview of the Obama International Tax Proposals." *Tax Notes*, June 15, 2009.

Sullivan, Martin A. "Cisco CEO Seeks Relief for Profits Shifted Overseas." *Tax Notes*, November 29, 2010.

Sullivan, Martin A. "Drug Company Profits Shift Out of United States." *Tax Notes*, March 10, 2010.

Sullivan, Martin A. "Extraordinary Profitability in Low-Tax Countries." *Tax Notes*, August 25, 2008.

Sullivan, Martin A. "Foreign Tax Credit Proposal Puts Brakes on Earnings Coming Home." *Tax Notes*, May 25, 2009.

Sullivan, Martin A. "Jobs and International Tax Rules." *Tax Notes*, February 10, 2010.

Sullivan, Martin A. "Medtronic Moves Jobs, Profits Out of U.S." *Tax Notes*, August 16, 2010.

Sullivan, Martin A. "Microsoft Moving Profits, Not Jobs, Out of the U.S." *Tax Notes*, October 18, 2010.

Sullivan, Martin A. "Offshore Jobs and Taxes: Will Democrats Attack?" *Tax Notes*, April 7, 2008.

Sullivan, Martin A. "Oil Drillers Gain Billions from 'Immoral' Tax Break." *Tax Notes*, June 14, 2010.

Sullivan, Martin A. "Repatriation Holiday Would Destroy American Jobs." *Tax Notes*, November 15, 2010.

Sullivan, Martin A. "Should the U.S. Limit 'Excessive' Returns in Low-Tax Countries?" *Tax Notes*, March 15, 2010.

Sullivan, Martin A. "'Stateless Income' Is Key to International Reform." *Tax Notes*, June 27, 2011.

Sullivan, Martin A. "The Politics of Hewlett-Packard Sending Jobs Offshore." *Tax Notes*, September 22, 2008.

Sullivan, Martin A. "Time to Scrap the Research Credit." *Tax Notes*, February 22, 2010.

Sullivan, Martin A. "Transfer Pricing Abuse Is Job-Killing Corporate Welfare." *Tax Notes*, August 2, 2010.

Sullivan, Martin A. "Transfer Pricing Costs U.S. at Least $28 Billion." *Tax Notes*, March 22, 2010.

Sullivan, Martin A. "U.S. Drug Firms Bring Home $98 Billion." *Tax Notes*, April 17, 2006.

Sullivan, Martin A. "U.S. Multinationals Cut U.S. Jobs While Expanding Abroad." *Tax Notes*, September 13, 2010.

Sullivan, Martin A. "U.S. Multinationals Moving Jobs to Low-Tax, Low-Wage Countries." *Tax Notes*, April 14, 2008.

Sullivan, Martin A. "U.S. Multinationals Shifting Profits Out of the United States." *Tax Notes*, March 10, 2008.

Sullivan, Martin A. "Why Not an Investment Credit for Overseas Operations?" *Tax Notes*, March 14, 2011.

Sullivan, Martin A. "Will Obama's International Proposals Kill U.S. Jobs?." *Tax Notes*, June 1, 2009.

State Corporate Tax

Brunori, David. *State Tax Policy: A Political Perspective, Second Edition*. Washington DC: Urban Institute Press, 2006.

Sullivan, Martin A. "Business Tax Reform: Lessons From Texas." *Tax Notes*, May 5, 2008.

Sullivan, Martin A. "Congress Must Act to Streamline State Corporate Taxes." *Tax Notes*, October 4, 2010.

Sullivan, Martin A. "State Tax Incentives—Who Will Clean Up the Mess?" *Tax Notes*, April 10, 2006.

Pass-Through Entities

Borden, Bradley T. "Three Cheers for Passthrough Taxation." *Tax Notes*, June 27, 2011.

Joint Committee on Taxation. Tax Reform: Selected Federal Tax Issues Relating to Small Business and Choice of Entity. JCX-48-08, June 4, 2008.

Keightley, Mark P. "Business Organizational Choices: Taxation and Responses to Legislative Changes." Congressional Research Service Report for Congress, August 6, 2009.

Sullivan, Martin A. "Passthroughs Shrink the Corporate Tax by $140 Billion." *Tax Notes*, February 28, 2011.

Sullivan, Martin A. "Why Not Tax Large Passthroughs as Corporations?" *Tax Notes*, June 6, 2011.

Government Accountability Office. "Tax Policy: Summary of Estimates of the Costs of the Federal Tax System." GAO-05-878, August 26, 2005.

Simplification

Lobel, Martin. "Simplifying the Tax System Will Help Our Economy," in *Toward Tax Reform: Recommendations for President Obama's Task Force.* Tax Analysts, 2010, http://www.tax.org.

Moore, Kevin B. "The Effects of the 1986 and 1993 Tax Reforms on Self-Employment." Board of Governors of the Federal Reserve System, Finance and Economics Discussion Series 2004–05, 2004.

Plesko, George A. "Gimme Shelter? Closely Held Corporations since Tax Reform," National Tax Journal, September 1995.

Slemrod, Joel and Marsha Blumenthal, "The Income Tax Compliance Cost of Big Business." *Public Finance Quarterly*, October 1996.

Slemrod, Joel and Varsha Venkatesh. "The Income Tax Compliance Cost of Large and Mid-Size Business." Report to the IRS LMSB Division, Internal Revenue Service, 2002.

Slemrod, Joel. "The Economics of Corporate Tax Selfishness." NBER Working Paper No. 10858, October 2004.

Federal Budget

Burman, Leonard E., Jeff Rohaly, Joseph Rosenberg, and Katherine C. Lim. "Catastrophic Budget Failure." *National Tax Journal*, September 2010.

Congressional Budget Office. CBO's 2011 Long-Term Budget Outlook. June 2011.

Reinhart, Carmen and Kenneth Rogoff. *This Time Is Different: Eight Centuries of Financial Folly*. Princeton, NJ: Princeton University Press, 2009.

Sullivan, Martin A. "A National Debt Headed off the Charts." *Tax Notes*, March 30, 2009.

Sullivan, Martin A. "Business Should Lead on Deficit Control and Tax Reform." *Tax Notes*, July 5, 2010.

Sullivan, Martin A. "Congressional Numbers Hide U.S. Debt Explosion." *Tax Notes*, May 4, 2009.

Sullivan, Martin A. "Fiscal Crisis, Part 1: The Slow Descent to Second-Class Status." *Tax Notes*, November 1, 2010.

Sullivan, Martin A. "Fiscal Crisis, Part 2: Catastrophe." *Tax Notes*, November 7, 2010.

Sullivan, Martin A. "Notes on the British Austerity Budget." *Tax Notes*, September 20, 2010.

Sullivan, Martin A. "Replace Pay-Go With Debt-to-GDP Targeting." *Tax Notes*, March 16, 2009.

Sullivan, Martin A. "Ryan's Rocky Roadmap to Fiscal Responsibility." *Tax Notes*, May 31, 2010.

Sullivan, Martin A. "The Federal Debt: Why Sustainability Is Not Enough." *Tax Notes*, July 6, 2009.

Index